SHEMSU-HOR

EDOUARD PONIST

authorHOUSE

AuthorHouse™
1663 Liberty Drive
Bloomington, IN 47403
www.authorhouse.com
Phone: 833-262-8899

Published by AuthorHouse 11/19/2021

ISBN: 978-1-6655-4392-7 (sc)
ISBN: 978-1-6655-4391-0 (e)

To my wife Laurel Ponist, Sara ONeil and grandchildren
Finbar and Grace, Alison Seaton and grandchildren
Andrew and Esme, Jack Porter, with love.

Special thanks
to Graham Hancock who was central to my curiosity and
quest, opening a different way of seeing the historical
past and his wife Santha whose splendid pictures
are found in Graham's books.

CONTENTS

INTRODUCTION

Two cultures, one very much alive, the other dead and separated by time. Yet each shares something which points to a common link very deep in the past.

A past was illuminated by an elite group of people who replaced chaos with order, ignorance with knowledge.

They were the Shemsu-Hor.

The Shemsu-Hor, also known as the Followers of Horus who "bear with them the knowledge of "divine origin" and unify the country with it..." (1) belong to an Ancient Egyptian myth. The Shemsu-Hor were half "gods" who gleaned information from the original Builder Gods who escaped a cataclysmic event. But out of the myth comes forth the truth and this truth points to a group of people who guided the select few. These elected people were given the blueprints encompassing spiritual, technical and linguistic skills. As the layers of cultures are peeled back and compared, linkages start to appear revealing a common thread between them.

What I discovered is a spiritual ritual used by the Hopis which can be found in an ancient Egyptian ritual as well. Like most discoveries, this one was purely accidental. This discovery leads to other similar links which will further strengthen the hypothesis that knowledge was preserved and disseminated by an elite group of survivors from an ancient land devastated by a cataclysm.

Plato suggested that periodically mankind starts anew as children without a recollection of the past. (2). These children seemed to be led by beings who guided them spiritually while giving them also the necessary tools needed for survival. Yet, throughout myth stories, there is a trend which repeats itself constantly. This trend is found in the constant reminder by these beings to adhere to a spiritual path and incorporate this path in everyday life. Dire consequences are threatened if a deviation from the spiritual path is taken. For example, the Hopi Ceremonial Calendar revolves around an agricultural way of life.

"the religion of the Hopi Indians of Arizona can be classified as a fertility religion with strong emphasis placed upon the gods of natural phenomenon and spirits of the dead." (3). The threat of crop losses looms, however, if ceremony is not performed with the proper focus, intent. The Hopi Indians take their ceremonials extremely seriously to the point, recently, of excluding outsiders from witnessing many ceremonies including the Snake Dance.

So long gone are the days when anthropologists such as Voth witnessed and photographed ceremonies and altars in kivas such as it was during the early 1900's.

It appears, based on the different myths and comments made by Plato, that the cataclysm which wiped out a prior civilization was sudden and complete. Graham Hancock has concluded that the object of that destruction was a comet.

Clues as to the comet can be found in Ancient Egyptian practices relating to meteorites used for ceremonial purposes. The Skidi Pawnee Indians used meteorites in their medicine bundles. It seems, actually, a worldwide phenomenon of fascination which brings people to flock towards these unwelcomed visitors from space.

The heart of my discovery begins with reeds. Relating to the Hopi, "The origin of the ceremonial and its objects and songs is to be found in the many myths concerning the founding of the secret societies. These myths are told in connection with the protomyth, i.e. the Emergence. But already in the Emergence Myth it becomes clear that certain objects, rituals, and ceremonials were present in the subterranean third world. Thus, according to the version told by the Kwaakwant, the entire emergence event happened during the execution of the Kwaakwant ceremonies on Wuwtsim initiation night. As long as their esoteric songs lasted, people were allowed to emerge. When the notes of the last song faded away, the vehicle of emergence, a giant reed, was knocked down, thereby denying the rest of mankind entrance to the new Fourth World." (4).

Keep this passage very much in mind when the protomyth of the Ancient Egyptians will be discussed.

Utterance 473 from the Ancient Egyptian Pyramid Texts is loaded with references to reeds, actually reed-floats. As you will see, reeds play a prominent part in the protomyth of Ancient Egypt. The reed, being at the heart of the protomyth of these two cultures, will reveal a mysterious practice, no longer in existence in Egypt but very much alive with the Hopi Indians today. The link will point to an undeniable point of origin common to both cultures deep in the midst of time; evidence linked by the Shemsu-Hor.

The common thread of knowledge is found throughout the world in many cultures through their myths. The myths are persistent and state the same information, worldwide. The great flood is not proprietary information to the Old Testament, the Bible. Flood myths are found throughout various cultures of the world including the Hopis and Ancient Egyptians. Thus, the repeated story line, separated by thousands of miles no longer fits the "myth", "legend" category. Myth and legends are quickly dismissed by academics as cultural stories, devoid of truth. The problem with that thesis is that the myths, legends repeat themselves with a common event-a cataclysmic event destroyed a world, and the elect were chosen to be saved and relocated. Builder Gods help along the refugees with knowledge like Spider Woman, Maasaw, Kokopeli of the Hopis, Thoth and many other Builder Gods of the Ancient Egyptians. Throughout the world, massive monuments of stone were erected with mathematical precision, aligned with the stars. That was their signature for future generations.

CHAPTER ONE

UNWELCOMED VISITORS

[After] the blast of a meteorite such that [even] the gods fear Isis
Awoke pregnant by the seed of her brother Osiris! (1)

Meteors, comets, evoke, in mankind, a primal fear as if a memory, deep in
our genetic makeup awakens our mind to potential danger.

No such fear was seen as I saw people straining through their telescopes
at the planetarium at Michigan State University when Hale-Bopp visited
up in 1987. The comet attracted much curiosity. However that curiosity
would have been replaced be a fear beyond what was shown in the movie
Deep Impact if it had taken earth in its sights.

On a wind swept observation area at Meteor Crater during the month
of May 1994, Graham Hancock, his wife Santha and myself examined
the results of what a meteor can do to the landscape. The crater reminded
me of a nuclear ground burst effect, except that this was bigger. Graham,
bracing himself against the wind walked around and periodically dictated
into his portable tape recorder. Later, in the museum, Graham pointed out
the orientation of one of the larger pieces recovered. Then we left, heading
towards Tuba City.

Much later, actually after Fingerprints of the Gods was published did
Graham venture a hypothesis: that the primary cataclysmic event which
destroyed an ancient civilization and triggered crustal displacement was,
perhaps, a comet or meteor which possibly impacted in the ocean. That event
could have very easily submerged that civilization, triggering massive volcanic
and earthquake activity. A nuclear winter would have set in setting off a

1

glaciation periood which suddenly thawed. With the thaw and subsequent rains, dry areas got flooded. Then over time land masses appeared.

Though the exact sequence of events may not have followed the above format, one thing is clear: throughout the world, a common theme runs through myths-that the world was completely destroyed by a flood by an angry god who was dissatisfied with humanity's sins.

In Message of the Sphinx, Graham Hancock and Robert Bauval link the fiery Phoenix bird of Ancient Egyptian myth with meteors. There is most definitely a transformational quality related to the effects of a comet strike. It changes everything on the surface of the planet. Furthermore, its effect would, today, instantly reset our civilization clock backwards.

I believe that post cataclysm, certain people were sent to different sites with specific missions. For example, let's look at the Hopi. After much traveling across water, guided by Spider Woman, the Hopi ancestors arrived at a land deemed by Spider Woman as adequate: it was not too lush, not too comfortable, designed to force people not to forget their spiritual duties. One of the most sacred ceremonial Hopi objects is the Tiiponi:

"It is a very sacred object, since it was first obtained in the Underworld during mythical times. It is the mother of the people, the heart of the clan, the society palladium. It is sometimes addressed as mother. Actually, it is a perfectly formed ear of white corn. When it is unwrapped (which occurs during a ceremonial) it is revealed to be an ear of corn set into a hollow base. The base contains seeds of various edible vegetables and is painted with cloud symbols on the four sides." (2).

The Hopis make up an agricultural, matriarchal society. The Hopi women own the land, the men cultivate it. The Hopis are superb agriculturists; once, while driving through Hopi lands, I saw beautiful corn plants growing out of seemingly arid desert soil. Spider Woman and Maasaw taught them well.

I asked a Hopi farmer how the plants were so green and he explained that each corn plant seed is placed in this sponge like mass which retains water. Each plant is individually watered periodically.

Maasaw was instrumental in providing spiritual guidance to the Hopi people. However, dire consequences would befall mankind if those teachings were to be forgotten. "When this story is forgotten," (referring to the handing over to the Hopi the stone tablets with Maasaw's inscribed instructions by Maasaw himself) "something disastrous will happen. Perhaps the stars will fall down in the ocean, and the ocean will become oil. Then the sun will set fire to it, and the conflagration will consume everyone. Perhaps there will be an earthquake that will kill everyone." (3). Modern Hopis interpret the qootsaptanga (jar of ashes) as a nuclear weapon. I don't agree. The reference refers one jar of ashes, not several. There is no weapon in the inventory that can cause, singly, the devastation described in the following text. "Text 158 They say that if in the future we deviate from the teachings given to us by the one who gave us the breath of life, and if we ignore our religious belief, thereby bringing ourselves to koyaanisqatsi or "life in turmoil", at that time our father will cast down upon us a jar of ashes as a result of which we will all perish. Thereupon the entire earth will go up in flames and all the seas will boil. (5). At that point life will cease to exist." (5) This prophetic warning is one of three prophesies chanted in Hopi, in Godfrey Reggio's movie Koyaanisqatsi. (4). Immediately following, text 159 tells us the following: "Our elders maintain that, according to an instruction from the one who owns this world, our existence cease by means of a jar of ashes, if we are unable to control ourselves. They also claim that he who gave us life will throw this jar, whereupon our lives will terminate. Since the jar contains nothing but extremely potent materials, no one will survive when he tosses it at us. And the shape of this earth as we know it will be totally destroyed." (5).

A jar has a large bottom and tapers towards the neck, just like a comet which has a rounded leading edge and tapers to what is referred to as the tail of the comet. I believe that the Qootsaptanga is a comet, a future event which will destroy again an unruly mankind. In The Mars Mystery Graham Hancock describes the worldwide fire storm which would be generated by a comet strike on earth. Furthermore, the boiling of water would fit what would occur if a comet impacted into the ocean; the water would vaporize and the hole created would fill in violently by the in rushing water. The churning would appear, from space, as boiling water. So in summary we have:

-One object
-Shaped like a jar
-Global destruction by fire
-Boiling seas

Which would suggest a comet strike in an ocean at a future time when man becomes disorderly again. Man's conduct today seems to fit uncomfortably that theme…

The disorderly Orderly. Yet, I believe it is a cosmic event which occurs at precise periodic times as earth navigates through space. It is a common theme in many spiritual scripts (Revelations, as an example) to pin the blame on mankind. The many spiritual edicts throughout the world want man to conform to a code of conduct which is essential for a society to exist. Chaos does not produce perfectly nurtured Hopi corn plants. Order must occur for mankind to exist.

Disturbingly, Maasaw describes what would be referred to as a nuclear winter; from "Text 154: Again, Maasaw added, "Then these light-skinned people with great talents will probably send someone to the moon. Next they will also experiment with the sun. But nothing will reach it, for anything which comes close will burn up. No one will be able to reach the sun. But its heat will most likely be exploited. Then the sun won't be as hot anymore, and the summer season will grow shorter and shorter. One day the weather will no longer get warm. You will experience snowfall at the height of planting time. To sow, the farmer will have to push aside the snow, dig a hole, and plant his seeds. It will come to this if you extract those precious things from the earth."

"And all the grasses across the land, which many different animals feed on to raise their young, will not grow as before. In the future the animals will suffer great hardships when these grasses do not sprout. There will be no point in having rain, for when the warmth is gone, nothing will grow as it used to."

"Gradually your corn plants will only produce tassels and then everything will freeze. And when you replant, only tiny, stunted ears will appear, and then they too will freeze. The third time you sow, the stalks will still be short before the frost strikes. By the fourth time the plants will barely have pierced the earth before freezing. At that time you will come to a time of famine." All these predictions Maasaw made to the Hopi." (6).

It is not clear if the freezing will occur pre or post jar of ashes episode. What is clear is that post comet strike, after the fires subside, a pall of debris and smoke would block the sun's rays for years creating a winter like environment on the earth destroying any means to plant and grow crops. Whoever survived the fires would die, eventually, of cold and starvation.

The reference to experimentation with the sun strikes me as interesting. Wallace Black Elk states that the sun is an abode to Tunkashila, a "Lakota referring to the Grandfather or male aspect of the Creator." (7). A spirit instructed Black Elk thus: "And he said. I'm a spirit. Tunkashila sent me here. I'm a spirit. Tunkashila sent me here. And there are four holes in that sun, and inside that sun there is a land. No one is to touch that fire (nuclear energy). That same fire was placed here, and man was not to touch it, because it's sacred. But when man discovered that fire, he made a destructive tool with it, so man will destroy himself." (8).

Nuclear energy, on this planet, mimics the sun's power, here on earth. Though we know that the sun's power is nuclear, nothing more is really known of the sun. Sure, we know that the sun produces sun flares and that there are periodic solar activities which can be measured. Other than that, the sun is a great mystery. It is a giver of life; without the sun, all life would cease. The sun gives us freely its energy for mankind to use appropriately. However, what if man uses Tunkashila's energy in the wrong way? What if the sun's energy was utilized to destroy? Would that act be an affront to the Creator seated in the sun? Would that gift be thus taken away as a lesson to never use Tunkashila's energy wrongly? And would we ever learn that lesson in the far future if survivors made it through the ordeal of the sun's brief extinction?

A stellar interest is also found with the Skidi Pawnee Indians. However, I would like to first quote part of Utterance 466 of the Ancient Egyptian Pyramid Texts:

The king becomes a star

O King, you are this great star, the companion of Orion, who traverses the sky with Orion, who navigates the Netherworld with Osiris; you ascend from the east of the sky, being renewed at your due season and rejuvenated at your due time. The sky has borne you with Orion….(9).

The Skidi Pawnee made use of an earth lodge in which a Skidi priest made careful observations of the planets and stars. "The surviving list of planets, stars, and constellations indicates that the Skidi had a well-developed system of labeling objects of the sky. Records on the Skidi have mentioned five planets, two dozen individual stars, and about fifteen constellations. Only a few of these are clearly identified. The Skidi were among the few native tribes to have made a chart of the sky." (9).

What is also curious about the Skidi Pawnee is that they considered meteorites sacred and if found were kept in sacred medicine bundles. The people believed that as long as the meteorites were in their possession, success in all things would occur. The following quote closely parallels the Ark of the Covenant's power and its ability to induce visions and communication with God:

"The Skidi also have in their keeping meteorites or stones that have fallen from the skies. They are considered the children of Tirawahat and are supposed to have great powers. These precious stones are wrapped up thickly with various kinds of handkerchiefs and are only taken out when someone has had a dream about them." (101).

But what is stunning is the close alignment made with utterance 466 from the Pyramid Text quoted above with the following:

"My grandchild, some of the signs have come to pass. The stars have fallen among the people but the Morning Star is good to us, for we continue to live....Our people were made by the stars. When the time comes all things to end our people will turn into small stars and will fly to the South Star, where they belong. When the time comes for the ending of the world the stars will again fall to the earth. They will mix among the people, for it will be a message to the people to get ready to be turned into stars." (11).

Though the South Star is not Orion, the parallelism is quite chilling. In one, the king becomes a star, in the other, the people become stars. In both cultures, there is a strong stellar influence with a strong ritual associations with a star cult. In both cultures, meteorites, which can spell doom to humanity, are worshiped. And even more stunningly, "evidence suggests that the traditional Plains feather bonnet symbolized a comet." (12).

Coincidence or a common thread of knowledge running through cultures? And if it is a common thread of knowledge, then who made sure the knowledge was well distributed? Who made sure the knowledge was well blended in the existing cultures spread throughout the world?

It appears to me that someone was working from a master blueprint and sent messengers all over the world post cataclysm. These messengers shared a sacred knowledge brilliantly applied within the varied cultures and cleverly hidden behind ritual and ceremony. Sacred stories and legends were weaved within the ceremonies further encoding this sacred knowledge from those un initiated people who many have been and still considered evil and unworthy of such sacred gifts.

In her book The Sirius Connection, Murry Hope suggests that behind the veil of ritual and ceremony of Ancient Egypt lies the roots of an ancient science. However, time distorted the original meaning and as the gap of time grew the ceremony became more mechanical, routine. I feel, though, that today, there are a select few who really know the answers but will not reveal those answers to the non-initiated.

Graham Hancock, in the last chapter of Fingerprints of the Gods presents a scenario of how, over time, a technology became distorted, obscured, transformed into myths. Eventually, the original event became so distorted that it became impossible to identify this technology relative to a time when the myths became the focus of study. The original event, thus transformed lost credence as a real event in the minds of academics. The real event thus became fiction.

Recently, I asked my oldest daughter, Sara, what she would try to save if the earth was threatened by a comet strike. She responded that she would save music stored on CDs. These CDs would form a time capsule of our music for future generations.

I thought about this and the response just did not sit right with me. Not that the idea is wrong; far from it. Actually it was quite a noble response, tailored to our technology at this time.

But let us go forward in time with those CDs. How about five thousand years in the future. Where will we be? CDs are small and fragile. Will they withstand the rigors of time? Will anyone, if found, know what to do with them, or will they be used as Frisbees?

I believe that the Shemsu-Hor did two things: one, that an oral tradition was passed on with strict instructions that the tradition be transmitted verbatim without fail under penalty of dire consequences. The Navajo sand paintings used during their sings and the Hopi altars are examples of such tradition. Second, that massively huge and precisely aligned stone structures were built throughout the world as markers which Graham Hancock discusses in his book Heaven's Mirror.

Let's examine stone. Stone is about as permanent as any substance known to man. It is subjected to slow weathering. And if one builds a massive structure, it will last thousands of years.

The key here is thousands of years, not centuries. The builders would want to impress, on future generations, precision on a massive scale, in other words, build a book written in stone.

A book written in stone…just like the Great Pyramid in Egypt in which not an inscription is found engraved on its walls. A massive statement built out of massive blocks of stone precisely aligned north-south in order to tell future generations: "We have a message to give you."

There are many other such stone messengers all around the world. Stonehenge is another example. Much has been written about these messengers. But one should look at the stone.

The stone will give future generations a key. Sara's idea about saving our civilization's music on disc might work. However, a more daring idea would follow a different path:

A Shemsu-Hor would say: "Forget our music. We will, when things settle down, build a stone structure which incorporates mathematically the Golden Mean and other mathematical formulas. Future people who will know how to read the stone will write the formulas which, in turn, will be studied by learned men and women. There will be geniuses in the future who will be born and who will recognize harmony in those symbols. New music will be composed. New architecture will be erected. This future civilization will be built from the keys in those stones."

No one has found as of yet a chamber loaded with artifacts and scrolls from a lost civilization. It is quite possible no one ever will. The keys disclosing the secrets of that civilization however can be found in any major stone structure which dot the surface of this planet. Some of them are huge, evoking wonder. How were they built? Who built them?

I believe that they were built with purpose and durability in mind. There was also a shock effect built in as well like size and precision. They were built to impress and provoke questions. They weathered slowly…

Water is one of the most destructive solvents on this planet. As a life sustaining substance it has no equal. But its destructive power in the form of floods and violent rain rivals fire in its destructive ability.

If flooding was a direct or indirect result of a comet strike,that memory of the power of water lingered for a long time in the memory of those who survived its wrath. The memory of this flooding is universal. It follows myth upon myth like a bad dream.

There is evidence that pre-dynastic Egypt was a very wet place. The god Min belonged to a group of gods called the Storm Gods. Min's symbol was "the many-pointed weapon", "the light-weapon, the thunderbolt." (13). G.A. Wainwright adds that "Min wore the high feathers and streamer just as did Amun who was a god of the winds. His sacred animal was the bull, and bulls are common representatives of sky-gods in the Near East." (14).

Seth was also classified as a Storm God associated with Taurus (15) whose sacred animal was the hippopotamus. Iron, "the bone of Typhon" (16) confirmed "Petrie's discovery at Kaw (an important center of Seth worship) of great quantities of gigantic bones, collected in piles: they were chiefly of hippopotami – mineralized, heavy, black bones, of metallic luster and appearance. It is clear that they were considered sacred to Seth, as they were wrapped in linen and were found here and there in tombs at Kaw." (17). Further confirming the deep antiquity of thunderbolt imagery ""some 22 miles of the south-east of Letopolis, a number of faience and alabaster "thunderbolts "were found and also faience Horus falcons." (18). Letopolis was identified by Robert Bauval and Adrian Gilbert in The Orion Mystery as the center of the Opening of the Mouth Ceremony and a meteoric cult. (19). The "Thunderbolt City" known as such because of the thunderbolt symbol which "existed at Letopolis in pre-dynastic times, that is to say the time of the Decorated pottery." (20).

Besides the faience Horus Falcon found, a discovery of "a copper object showing the Horus falcon actually mounted on the "thunderbolt"" (21)

The Falcon mounted on a thunderbolt found near Letopolis, a city closely associated with the Opening of the Mouth Ceremony which was performed to sanctify the temple according to E.A.E. Raymond's work on the Edfu texts. (22) might reveal Letopolis as perhaps the site of the Primeval Mound of pre-dynastic history at the time of the great flood secondary to a comet strike which displaced the gods from their homeland.

A plain of reeds, a mound, emerging from a watery world; thunderbolts and meteoric iron. An emergence from the water, emerging from a dead world, an emergence to a place of reeds. The reeds presenting hope, life, a sacred memory of a lost world, an emergence tool fashioned into ceremonial implements and boats. A spiritual imperative, the first order of business by a people who were given a second chance, reborn into a new world, the fourth world of the Hopi, and the first time, Zep Tepi, of the Shemsu-Hor of pre-dynastic Egypt.

Rather viewing the ancient world as destroyed by an angry god as tradition dictates, one should examine the Gnostic point pf view which Graham Hancock outlines in his conclusion in Heaven's Mirror. The "collective amnesia" which Graham likes to portray humanity as a whole in relation to its past stems from a concerted effort by some to hide the truth, the light. By keeping mankind very busy materially, spirit can be easily extinguished. Knowledge of the past can only make us stronger, as we face the future as mature adults instead of the little children of Plato's commentary. As children, we are vulnerable to control. As rational, educated and enlightened adults we take control. However, it is as children that we can meet, and communicate with the Creator. But to maintain that spiritual child- like state we must constantly be vigilant to the dark side's attempt to destroy that state.

Knowing the past can prepare us for a future which may include an unwelcomed visitor striking our world.

The clues left in different cultures by a Shemsu-Hor points to a collective effort by a group to enlighten people at a crucial juncture in time. I believe that the time is fast approaching. The clues are presenting themselves in the most unusual places, in dissimilar settings. Their revelation seems almost planned...

There is evidence that the beginning of the Old Kingdom was lush with evidence of a savannah like environment as documented on stone. Water was plentiful yet something happened to the climate of Egypt near the end of Pepi IIs reign. Partly to blame for the decline was the delegation of power to governors by Pepi II yet a desertification of Egypt occurred causing massive famine. Possibly what occurred prior to Pre Dynastic Egypt caught up with Egypt itself plunging the Old Kingdom into chaos. Upper and Lower Egypt was eventually unified by the first historical pharaoh of Egypt who was Narmer.

CHAPTER TWO

SPIRITUAL IMPERATIVE

Hail clouds.

While reading H.R. Voth's exhaustive record of Hopi ceremonies and viewing his collection of photos all of which was done during the late 1800s, early 1900's, I felt deep sadness and a sense of loss. I feel that the exposure of sacred ceremonies signaled the twilight of Hopi spiritual paradise. I'm not implying that Hopis today are not spiritual people; in fact, they are fiercely so. However, the Hopi people are subjected to incredible pressures which have been building for many years. I got the feeling from a person named Melanie who had recently visited the Hopis that severe division has occurred in certain villages. Missionary pressure is as persistent as ever. Agricultural productivity is down related to changes in weather patterns. Disease is on the rise because of the proliferation of vermin also caused by weather changes. The Hopis are also getting pressure from innumerable seekers, some sincere, most not, who are looking for answers to vague needs and questions. Furthermore, the Hopis still are contending with land rights with the Navajo Tribe whose people persistently settle unwanted on Hopi land causing more tension between the two nations.

To blame also is the passive lukewarm interest of the United States Government. The Hopis represent an extremely rare society based on deep spiritual beliefs. The so called help and development has actually caused more damage to the culture. By not isolating the area and declaring it a historical site to be protected instead of being exploited has allowed a deterioration of Hopi culture. And this can be said about all other North American Indian tribes as well.

Am I being too harsh? Perhaps. However, this is not to say that positive institutions such as Indian Health Service should not have been allowed to form. Indian Health Service is today a powerful organization nationwide which provides excellent health care to the American Indian population. Having worked briefly as an Indian Health Service Nurse, I have seen first hand that the medical facilities work closely with native healers and medicine men. I have witnessed much positive influence that modern medicine has provided to the Navajo and Hopi population. I also have seen how western nutrition and alcohol has risen the specter of diabetes, coronary heart disease and obesity. However, I have also seen traditional members maintain traditional diets and way of life, keeping, in the process, healthy and active. But western diets and technology are seductive, contributing to an erosion of the traditional life-style.

One might say that this book is an example of profiteering by writing about Hopi sacred ways. Firstly, the information presented herein is already known by its publication in different sources; it's a matter of public record. Second, the knowledge that a link exists between two dissimilar cultures which points to an ancient knowledge in the deep past is important for all of us; as human beings, we need to understand and learn more about the remote past. Third, in order to know the future we must know the past in order that we, as human beings, can better prepare spiritually and materially to face possible severe future events.

Two cultures, one extinct, the other very much alive share a ceremonial practice which points to not a common origin but to a common gnosis, or sacred knowledge in the deep, remote past. We begin our journey by exploring the Hopi Altars.

Cosmic Platform

The Hopi Altar has a basic configuration which is not static but changes slightly depending on the ceremony performed. Subtle changes can be found during its construction and during the actual application of the altar during ceremonials.

There are four basic fields to the Hopi altar: "the first field consists of the altar frame, boards and idols; the second field consists of the sand ridge with its respective objects; the third field consists of the medicine altar and other instruments; and the fourth field consist of the sand mosaic." (1).

The sand ridge is an area of interest –

It represents, symbolizes the earth. (2).

Interestingly –

"A number of altars have a similar mosaic of raining clouds which, it should be noted, have rain falling towards the sand ridge of the altar. (3)

The rain falling on the sand ridge insures, ceremoniously life giving rain on the earth guaranteeing a successful crop.

But doesn't the sand ridge somewhat resemble the primeval mound of the Egyptian First Time? And the paahos stuck upright on the mound… don't they look like reeds…

Earlier, I mentioned that the Hopis make up an agricultural society as handed down by their ancestors. Legends relating to Maasaw, a Thoth like personage who possessed a vast knowledge, especially related to agriculture, possessed an impressive array of seeds, some magical, like the purple corn he carried around his waist which defied the severest weather (4), have set the Hopi society today as supreme agriculturists whose ceremonials revolve around the continuation of rain.

I already mentioned that Spider Woman, who led the original people made sure that the land on which the people settled was not too lush so that the people would remain faithful to their spiritual duties. And because the land was harsh, water was extremely important.

Maasaw, Spider Woman were Builder Gods. The word Gods, just like the Ancient Egyptian Gods, also Builder Gods represents to me very special people with unusual abilities and knowledge, survivors of a destroyed civilization whose job was to guide other survivors to a new settlement with all the knowledge necessary for survival. The Builder Gods also built in many parts of the world stone structures with hidden mathematical message. Those structures were designed to leave a message to future generations to decode, because destruction world again re-visit, a warning to future Builder Gods.

Water today is still very important in guaranteeing successful crops. The altar ceremonials tie in which ritual drama during different seasons of the Hopi calendar and astronomical observations. Failure during the performance of these ceremonials can spell crop failures. At a time before western influence, that failure would have spelled famine and death.

Today, with the advent of "Anglo" food supplies and a very diversified income producing base such as jewelry and Kachina "dolls" famine, as it was when the Hopi directly depended on their crops, is a moot point. However, the Hopi preserve their agricultural heritage as a cash crop and as a ceremonial crop in the form of corn. This way of life is central to the Hopi raison d'etre. It defines who the Hopi is and his relationship with the Creator. This relationship extends to the sacred beings, the Kachinas who are represented during the ceremonial dramas.

Water is an important element introduced during the construction of the altars. A key field is the Medicine Altar which Geertz defines as "the centripetal focal point for man and god alike." (5). Water is introduced in each four sides of the Medicine Bowl during the Medicine Altar Ritual which "transforms the medicine altar into a surrogate Sipaapuni." (6). (The Sipaapuni is the emergence access which the chosen people from the third world took "though the inner portion of the reed and finally climbed out into this world. (7), the Fourth World).

In this manner, "the altar and its kiva becomes a ritualized world center." (8).

The Medicine Bowl itself, being a surrogate Sipaapuni, "is a gateway through which the denizens of the spirit world can pass into the dimensions of physical reality." (9). Geertz further states that "The medicine bowl is the projector, so to speak." (10), a star gate to another dimension where the spirits and gods reside.

A ritual called the Medicine Altar ritual was recorded by Voth which is transcribed in its entirety in the end notes. (The Oraibi Marau Ceremony – Voth) (11). A part of that ritual is of great significance to the thesis of this book. But before examining that part of the Medicine Altar Ritual, Geertz states the following relating to water and the role of the dead: relating to the Snake-Antelope Ceremonial "Concerning rain: There are a number of powerful elements in this altar which can bring rain. The mosaic is the most obvious instrument, with its clouds raining upon the sand ridge, and its lightening snakes flashing overhead – a true summer thunderstorm. A pootavi is laid across the mosaic to facilitate the passage of the rain-bearing deities." (A pootavi "is a string with a down feather attached and which is placed on the ground and considered to be a road upon which clouds, deities, and spirits can travel" (12).

"Besides the water of the medicine bowl, water is doubly symbolized by the presence of another medicine bowl set into the sand ridge. The fact that it is set into the ridge suggests a cistern or well. To the right of the six directions altar is a cloud blower. Concerning the role of the dead and the founding of the society: all of the crooks and sticks lining the sides of the mosaic represent those society members who have passed away. The paahos "(which are specifiers "with a coded message which the elements or the gods can read." (13). (A Paaho is also known as a prayer stick, usually made of wood, painted, with feathers and gifts attached.) "which are lined up behind the bowl in the sand ridge, are constructed with a tsotsokpi or perch, i.e. the same type placed at the graves to facilitate the journey of the soul. Note that the feathers of these paahos lay upon the water of the bowl, indicating that the dead have power over rain." (14).

The Medicine Altar Ceremony observed by Voth contains the same information with a different twist: "The singing is then resumed, the woman beating time with one end of the stick on the floor. This stick, as well as the others in the sand ridge, is supposed to represent one of the dead members of the order (as is also the case with similar sticks in other ceremonies), and it is believed that the striking of the floor announces to the deceased members in the nether world that a ceremony is in progress." (as described in the Oaraibi Marau Ceremony, in part relating to the Medicine Altar Ceremony, (11)).

"the dead have power over rain." And the paahos built with a perch to facilitate the soul to perch upon during the ceremonial...

Keep this very much in mind when we will visit the Edfu Texts describing an event which was performed by the gods of Zep Tepi.

One disturbing document I must include here further enforces the perch, or seat theme for the soul. It is disturbing for several reasons: first, the Hopi are not comfortable with death. The same applies with the Navajo. So everything written about death rites would be regarded with distaste today by the Hopi people. Second, Voth, in this document, included pictures which are circular which indicates to me that they were taken secretly. This would, today, in anthropological circles to be the kiss of death to any academic research. Yet, the document exists, and is part of public record. The secrecy of taking pictures is a hypothesis of mine based on the circular picture which hints at a camera masking. I would like to, however, express to the Hopi people that the following quote is not meant to spell disrespect towards the Hopi death rites. And I hope that any researcher in the future will never ask to reproduce the pictures included in the Voth document to support his or her research. These photos should remain quietly in a book or archives and be viewed respectfully.

Voth describes a burial rite which included the mention of a perch, or seat for the departed soul. "The father, brother, or uncle of the deceased, that has prepared the remains for burial, now makes one double green baho (prayer stick, with black points), one single black baho, called chochokpi (seat), a puhu (road), consisting of an eagle breath feather. To this are tied two cotton strings, a shorter one, twisted several times, the other a single thread, but somewhat longer. Besides this he makes about six nakwakwosis." (The nakwakwosi is an eagle down feather to which a cotton string is attached. (15). "All this the one who makes the prayer offerings takes to the grave (see plate XXXIX) towards evening and places the two prayer sticks, the nakwakwosis, some corn-meal and the bowl with food on the grave (see Plate XL), the road he places on the ground west of the grave, the thin string pointing westward. From this road he sprinkles a meal line westward denoting the continuation of the road. According to a belief of the Hopi the hikvsi (breath or soul) of the deceased ascends early the next morning from the grave, partakes of the hikvsi of the food, mounts the hikvsi of the seat and then travels along the road to the masski (sleleton house) taking the hikvsi of the double baho along as an offering," (16).

In summary:

-Voth states in this paper that the adult Hopi is buried seated facing the east.

-The relative establishes the road west of the grave, with the string of the nakwakwosis pointing towards the west.

-The relative establishes the continuity of the road with corn meal, extending it westward.

-Except for children not initiated into a society, their roads leads back towards the home where the soul of the child will reside until it reincarnates "in the next child that is born in that family." (17).

The sun rises in the east, travelling westward during the day, just like the Boat of Millions of Years of Ancient Egypt. As E.A. Wallis Budge described the sacred boat's passage:

"the priests of Ra declared that the souls of the blessed made their way after death to the boat of Ra, and that they succeeded in alighting upon it their eternal happiness was assured. No friends could vex and no foes assail them successfully, so long as they had their seat in the "Boat of Millions of Years;" they lived upon the food on which the gods lived, and that food was light. They were apparelled in light, and they were embraced by the god of light. They passed with Ra in his boat through all dangers of the Tuat," (commonly called the underworld, but according to Budge the meaning of the Tuat is unknown) "and when the god rose each morning they were free to wander about in heaven or to visit their old familiar habitations on earth, always however taking care to resume their places in the boat before nightfall, at which time evil spirits had great power to injure, and perhaps even to slay, the souls of those who had failed to arrive safely in the boat." (18).

The deceased Hopi faces the rising sun, the residence of Tunkashila of the Lakota; the solar bark ascends in the sky. The western road established the previous evening acts as a marker for the soul which ascends early the next morning and mounts the soul of the seat, the chochokpi. The soul then proceeds along the road bearing gifts to the "skeleton house" then travels westward, following the course of the sun; may it be that the skeleton house is the solar bark of Ra, the Supreme Creator that the Ancient Egyptians believed to reside in the sun, just like the Lakota belief as expressed by Wallace Black Elk.

Per Shannon Austin, "In 108 Sun Salutations, Heated Yoga, Hot Yoga benefits" "What is the significance of 108 in Yoga?"

"Why the number 108? The number 108 is considered a sacred number in Hinduism, Buddhism and yogic tradition. Malas or Japa beads come in a string of 108 and are used for devotional meditation, mantra and prayer. With each bead a mantra or prayer is repeated to meet a total of the 108. The Meru bead is the larger bead or tassel on the mala and is not part of the 108. This is the guiding bead and marks the beginning and end of the mala/chant/prayer/mantra."

"Here are a few interpretations of the significance of the number 108.

Sanskrit alphabet has 54 letters. Each letter has a masculine (Shiva) and feminine (Shakti) energy 54X2=108.

Desires. There are said to be 108 earthly desires in mortals.

17

Time. It is said we have 108 feelings. 36 related to the past, 36 related to the present, 36 related to the future.

Astrology. There are 12 constellations and 9 arc segments. There are 12 houses and 9 planets. 12X9=108.

The diameter of the sun is 108 times the earth."

In the chapter The Osiris Number, Chapter 31, Fingerprints of the Gods by Graham Hancock, Graham states-"The pre-eminent number in the code is 72. To this is frequently added 36, making 108, and it is permissible to multiply 108 by 100 to get 10,800 or to divide it by 2 to get 54, which may then be multiplied by 10 and expressed as 540(or as 54,000, or as 540,000, or as 5,400,000, and so on).Also highly significant is 2160 (the number of years required for the equinoctial point to transit one zodiacal constellation), which is sometimes multiplied by 10 and by factors of ten (to give 216,000, 2,160,000, and so on) and sometimes by 2 to give 4320, or 43,200, or 432,000, or 4,320,000, ad infinition."

The number 72 "equals the number of years required for the equinoctial sun to complete a precessional shift of one degree in the ecliptic;" (Fingerprints of the Gods Chapter 31, Graham Hancock).

Why am I bringing this up? Sacred numbers-To Hinduism and Buddhism, and Ancient Egypt; 108. The Sun had great significance to the Ancient Egyptians. The Boat of a Million Years travels East to West. The Hopi relative marks the path for the soul towards the West. The "Skeleton House", the Solar Boat? The connection between the Hopis and Tibet…Tibetan Lamas and the Dalai Lama have had numerous dialogues with the Pueblo and Hopi Indians…

Lets go back to the paahos on the sand ridge constructed with a tsotsokpi, as described by Geertz, and the sticks in the sand ridge as described by Voth on which perches the souls of the dead who have power over the rain. "Crook-shaped wooden wands have been used in prehistoric times and are also employed at the present for use in ceremonies" (Hough, Walter; 1914, pp. 93-95.), the purpose of which are largely connected with petitions for rain and fertility. These wands are often adorned with feathers and as there seems to have some belief which conceived birds as prayer bearers, it may be plausible to think of the crook, and allied ceremonial objects having the general form, as derived from a similar idea as that associated with the simple bird forms found on pottery." (19). H.P. Mera further states that certain paraphernalia such as crooks, drumsticks, bows and feathers are associated with prayers beseeching rain. (20).

The bird, associated with wooden sticks appears to be a symbol of the soul, just like the Ba of Ancient Egypt. However, the bird/soul is again associated with rain. The only difference is that the Ba was represented with a bird's body and the face of a human being. No such analogy can be made with the birds depicted on Pueblo pottery. The wands that Mara refers to closely resembles the paaho/tsotsokpi assembly of the Hopi altar. The wands, associated with feathers, therefore associated with birds, would follow the logic that, the tsotsokpi being a perch for the souls of the dead during ceremonials, the bird is a symbolic representation of the human soul using the wands as a platform, or perch.

The Hopi altar is truly a cosmic platform, a stargate coaxing departed souls of past members of a society into the kiva and onto their respective perch. The ceremonials and ritual drams enacted create an energy field which attracts life giving rain. The perch concept extends to the seat for the soul of a departed Hopi at his or her burial site. Facing east, the soul waits until the sun rises the next morning then takes flight, perches momentarily then proceeds with gifts westward, following the sun, with which it meets, just like the souls who embark on the Boat of Millions of Years, the solar bark of Ra, the Creator.

Even though much was written on the Hopi altars, much yet still remains a mystery. Detailed descriptions and photographs still do not reveal the inner secrets of the Hopi ceremonialism. I doubt anthropologists will ever penetrate these inner secrets because, like most spiritual secrets, their revelation begin through an internal, personal experience. To be privy to this experience one must be a Hopi.

I suspect, though, that part of the inner secrets concerns stellar issues. For example, when I went to South Dakota several years ago on a research project for Graham Hancock, I discovered a small pamphlet titled Lakota Star Knowledge by Ronald Goodman. This pamphlet was petitioned by the Lakota to be banned from future publication. My interview with Ron revealed serious backpedaling on this subject. This censorship stemmed from a deep anger from Lakota initiates towards this pamphlet. I learned, from my interview with Ron that the pamphlet touched the very periphery of Lakota star knowledge yet it touched off a reaction leading to the censorship of the pamphlet. Today, myself and Graham have a pamphlet each. They probably are two of very few held in non Lakota hands at present.

As I mentioned earlier, star knowledge is also found with the Skidi Pawnee Indians. Star knowledge being such a sensitive issue with the Lakota, it follows, logically, that is must be found in other spiritual beliefs of other tribes as well.

The Hopi altar appears to be a cosmic platform, a stargate, through which initiated members tap into ceremonies which I believe are star related. The only evidence I'm basing this is the strong reaction by the Lakota relating to any information leaked about their star cult which is very secret indeed.

Is it important for us to know? Some things are not meant to be revealed until the time comes to reveal them. Anthropology today has evolved to a point that some sacred knowledge must be left alone if the subjects are unwilling to reveal it. However, there are still researchers out there who will attempt to probe those inner secrets. The saving grace is that they are of the wrong ethnic, cultural and religious background. They don't possess a "passport" to this knowledge. Regardless of their efforts, they will be blocked and pacified by driblets of information that is pretty much common knowledge.

Possessing 14 pounds of plutonium does not mean one can build a nuclear weapon; knowledge and acquisition of many parts are necessary to assemble a complete weapon.

Sometimes one has to step back away from interviews and documentation and just observe. By stepping back, revelations may begin to surface through deep observation and reflection. But be prepared. When the truth will reveal itself, you may not be willing to reveal anything at all…

Temple Builders

"The slip of reed is the name of the Perch in Wetjeset-Neter. Thus Djeba <in> Wetjeset-Neter became the name of this domain great being the water flood <in> the fields that surround the region of reed." (21).

Djeba in Wetjeset-Neter was "a primitive sacred place" (22) where "the Falcon, also called Lord of Dejeba" (23) rested on a perch called the djeba-perch in a place of reeds. The Falcon, identified as "Horus the Behdetitie", :Lord of Dejeba", (24) was instructed secrets by the Ka, the deceased earth god (25) through a relic of a lost world of the gods, the dd pillar or djeba, also commonly known as the djed pillar. The wanderings by a strange group of gods identified as "the Ogdoad, Seshat, the Seven Builder Gods, Thoth and the Seven Sages" (26) established sacred residence on sacred mounds amidst an inundated land which included, as the first thing, the erection of a sacred link to the lost world, the djed pillar on which a perch of reed was constructed for the Falcon. Also known as the "Shebtiw" (27) this divine group was led by "the Two Companions of the Divine Heart", Wa and Aa (28).

The Shemsu-Hor, a builder elite, from a lost, destroyed world, established, before anything else a sacred residence for the Falcon/Horus who was the link to the Ka/spirit of the deceased earth god of the lost world which hints that the gods themselves were mortal, just mere human beings with very unusual abilities and knowledge from a lost world destroyed by water.

This also hints to a survivor group in deep antiquity who became, because of an antiquity hardly remembered, gods in the eyes of future generations wrapped with a story line which became legend and the basis of the spiritual doctrine of Ancient Egypt.

Authors such as Graham Hancock and Murry Hope have developed the hypothesis that in a very remote time, a powerful civilization thrived and was extinguished by a catastrophic event which scattered survivors all over the globe.

Archeologists such as Mark Lehner continuously drone the party line of academics demanding physical evidence of this lost civilization. Ironically, the evidence is in front of them in the form of complex stone structures around the globe containing mathematical models which Graham Hancock, Robert Bauval and Adrian Gilbert have presented in their brilliant books.

The Falcon on his perch on the djed pillar is well represented on page 275 in the Message of the Sphinx by Graham Hancock and Robert Bauval. Interestingly "the reed was the sole relic of the former domain of the Pn-God and his fellows," and that the reed "contained the power of uplifting the god; the relic of the early domain was the only means through which the dead world might have been brought to its former state. The reed was the material from which the dd-pillar was made, and as the relic of the first sacred world that vanished, provided the essential element for the creation of a new sacred domain that succeeded the former in a direct line." (29).

E.A.E. Raymond continued later by stating that "This first domain created at the dawn of the new period of creation bears the name of Wetjeset-Neter. The manner in which it was created proves that it assumed and bore the function and characteristics of its antecedent, the sacred domain of the dd-pillars that vanished. Then, after the Perch had been erected and the new divine being in the island had alighted upon it, the ancestral drty-Falcons were awakened from their slumber. They returned to the place where they formerly ruled in their spiritual forms. This is evident from the presence of the Soul described as the Flying BA." (30).

It is obvious that Reymond is interpreting legend and spiritual doctrine from the Edfu texts. However, a leap beyond established academic thought must be ventured.

Reymond brilliantly explored extremely ancient myth in her book, the Mythical Origin of the Egyptian Temple. But between the lines I sense a sacred science, a sacred knowledge which was shared by many cultures.

For example, the reed, so sacred to the Builder Gods was the means through which the Hopi ancestors emerged into the Fourth World. Utterance 473 of the Ancient Egyptian Pyramid Texts is loaded with reference to reed-floats; Spider Woman, who strangely resembles Isis, packed the elect from the Third World as instructed by Sotuknang in reeds with water and corn meal dough before the great flood occurred. Afterwards, the survivors used a giant reed to climb on in search of land. They continued their search of a land which needed approval by Spider Woman in reed boats. (31).

Another interesting link with reeds is the usage of flutes in many cultures throughout the world. The humpbacked flute player Kokopelli of the American Southwest rock art stretches that link to the depths of time to reeds. A memory of a lost world? And why is Kokopelli represented as a humpbacked individual? Dennis Slifer and James Duffield, in their book Kokopelli suggests a trade link with a possible link to sacks carried on backs by itinerant traders to the hump on Kokopelli's back. (32). It's possible. However, one must heed to Schwaller de Lucbicz's caution that a symbol carries a very deep meaning only known to initiates. I suspect that Kokopelli imagery means something entirely different to Hopi initiates today.

For example, if Kokopelli was a trader, then from where did he come from? Was he a humpbacked? What did the flute represent? What harmonic does the flute carry? What was Kokopelli represented so widely throughout the American Southwest? Why was he tied to phallic representations? Was he some kind of American Indian Pan? Why a flute and not a drum?

Back to the reed/flute analogy, it seems to me uncanny that such an instrument has such universal appeal. This universal trend appears to point to a common knowledge, a long long time ago.

Was the djed pillar a real object? Reymond suggests perhaps not, that "only the memory of it seems to have remained in the knowledge of the creators." (33). One thing is certain: Its power was immense and was prerequisite to the building of the temple. Its use as a communication device through which the Ka of the deceased earth god spoke secrets to the Falcon and its power over the primeval water was evident. After the Shebtiw restored the djed pillar, the primeval water receded; then the Ka gave specific instructions for the construction of the djeba-perch. Afterwards, the primeval water (the flood?) became calm. Worship, a silent rite and perhaps a protective rite was performed (34) afterwards.

Power over water…The Ka of the earth god having power over water, the dead members of the Hopi secret society, invited to perch on their tsotsokpi because of their power over rain.

The Shemsu-Hor wanted the water to recede; the Hopis want rain for their crops. Each application points to a common origin of thought and purpose.

What this origin might have been seems to be related to a stellar one. For example, the blueprint of the original Egyptian temple appears to have originated from the sky. "In a well-known text on the inner face of the enclosure wall of the temple of Edfu tells us that the temple was built at the dictates of the Ancestors according to what was written in this book which descended from the sky to the north of Memphis" (35).

The stellar theme is persistent in its message through the Giza Complex, Stonehenge, the Skidi Pawnee Star Lodge, the Lakota Star Knowledge; the astronomical data tell it all in the Message of the Sphinx and The Orion Mystery. The math does not lie. The math points to a knowledge that only star beings could know.

For example: in the Pyramid Texts, the king becomes a star in Orion and his bones become iron. (utterance 723, 738, 442 as an example. There are many other references to Orion and iron in the Pyramid Texts.) (36).

Sounds like something out of someone's fevered imagination who's been out in the sun too long…or not? When the Hubble Space Telescope sent back data to earth on Orion, it was discovered that Orion is a massive star factory. Furthermore, the National Geographic article on Orion of December 1995 reveals that: "In its old age a massive star converts helium to carbon and carbon to iron. It becomes a red supergiant, like old, bloated Betelgeuse, and when the nuclear furnace shuts off, gravity causes the star to collapse. The energy from this sudden contraction is released in a huge explosion, or supernova – a fate that no doubt will befall Betelgeuse."

"If the explosion occurs near a cloud of gas and dust, the shock waves may compress part of it. The gas becomes denser, and the star cycle begins anew." (37). Such a star "nursery" is the Orion Nebula.

How did the Ancient Egyptians know so much about Orion before the Hubble Space Telescope, or before any telescope for that matter…

The answer may lie in the prototypic temple of the First Time.

The first enclosure made of reeds which was the temple prototype, surrounding the djed pillar and the perch for the Falcon was the first act the Builder Gods accomplished upon arriving on the primeval mound and subsequent ones at year zero, the First Time. "It has been noticed that the dd pillar, as a resting place of a defunct deity, is always mentioned before the start of the new phase of creation. The dd pillar appears to determine the place in which the new sacred domain was to be created." (38). The djed pillar was a sacred relic which tied the Builder Gods thru the Falcon via the KA of the deceased earth god to the original, first domain which was destroyed. The Falcon temple being the simplest, the temple of the Sun-god was much more sophisticated in construction." (39). Its sanctity was insured through the ceremony of the Opening of the Mouth; "The magic power that was believed to have resided in the texts bearing on the mythical past of the temple imparted to it the mysterious life of the original sacred entity." (40). This reanimation of the temple transformed the temple into a living being. (41).

The Opening of the Mouth ceremony was a funerary ritual which E.A. Walls Budge detailed in The Book of Opening the Mouth. The Opening of the Mouth ceremony was also used in consecrating the Ancient Egyptian temple as described by E.A.E. Reymond in The Mythical Origin of the Egyptian temple. The paper by A.M. Blackman and H.W. Fairman titled The Consecration of an Egyptian Temple According to the use of Edfu (42) outlines in detail the Rite of Opening the Mouth as it was performed to awaken spiritually the temple. This act confirms that the temple was thought of as a living entity possessing a soul.

The strange meteoric iron implement called the meshtw was used during the Opening of the Mouth ritual. This instrument was also called the Adze of Upuaut, Upuaut being the Jackel-god. (43). The instrument's original meaning is fogged by time. Yet what is very interesting is that the shape of the meshtw resembles very closely the constellation of Ursa Minor as the German Egyptologist Bochardt stated. (44). I have to agree after examining Ursa Minor on a star map. The shafts from the King's Chamber and the Queen's Chamber in the Great Pyramid show northerly orientation, the King's shaft oriented to Alpha Draconis, the Queen's, oriented to Beta Ursa Minor. (45). They also strangely resemble the meshtw. Gantenbrink's small robot went up these shafts exploring. It was later that these northerly shafts were identified as appearing like the meshtw by Robert Bauval and Adrian Gilbert. (46).

The "thirteen stars in Draco beginning with Gamma and including two stars in Ursa Minor" (47) also known to the Lakota as Wakinyan or Thunderbird brings about an interesting link with the ancient headquarters headquarters of the Opening of the Mouth ceremony in Letopolis. Remember that Letopolis was the primary site of the Storm gods and the lightning bolt.

The Wakinyan come from the west draped in rain and lightning. The Sacred Pipe is regarded by the Lakota as the Wakinyan's sacred trust to the people. It was White Buffalo Calf Woman who brought the Sacred Pipe to the Lakota with instructions relating to the Seven Sacred Rites. If one really looks closely at an assembled Sacred Pipe (the red pipestone bowl attached to the slightly curved sumac stem) one would notice that it resembles Ursa Minor and the meshtw.

One afternoon, many years ago, my good friend Richard Seis gave me instruction on the Sacred Pipe in his lodge. I remember, while loading my Sacred Pipe, a sudden, violent thunderstorm which moved overhead very quickly. The storm, complete with lightning, thunder and rain, was gone by the time our small ceremony was complete. The Wakinyan visited us during this very special ceremony.

An interdimensional visit? A visit from the stars? I've learned since that with spiritual matters, acceptance, a letting go, rather than logical, rational explanations is the best course of action. Wallace Black Elk himself stated that the Sacred Pipe "is like a radio, like a radar. You could communicate from here directly to that main Chanunpa. You could communicate directly with the wisdom. Like I said, Tunkashila is the wisdom itself, and Grandmother is the knowledge." (48).

The original Chanunpa, or Sacred Pipe is held by the Lakota People. It is said that twelve eagle feathers are attached to the stem of the original Chanunpa (according to Ken Carey, in his book Return of the Bird Tribes) symbolically enforcing the link between the Sacred Pipe and the Thunderbeings.

There seems to be a universal gnosis shared by all cultures pointing to a common source, deep in antiquity. I believe that the source is stellar in origin. Yet, one must be careful in making that statement. The star beings were, and are today, deeply spiritual beings having a direct link to the Creator. That is why I believe space exploration will be denied to human beings until we evolve spiritually which in turn will reflect through our conduct in the physical world.

One might say "We have already explored our solar system with probes. We are on our way towards colonization." Not so fast. We are allowed to accomplish only what we can handle at this time. There are still deep racial and religious prejudices here on earth at present. We have polluted the earth to such an extent that major systems on earth are threatened at present, which are now starting to affect human beings as far as weather and crop failures. Human beings have not yet grasped the important link between the Creator and every day human affairs. Until we change our ways, space will be denied. In order for us to explore space, we must mature spiritually, way beyond where we are at present.

Yet, there is hope, because the spiritual gifts the Shemsu Hor gave mankind represent that optimism that human beings will, someday, get the message.

The temple of antiquity closely resembles the temple of our body. The physical temple, awakened by a consecration through the Opening of the Mouth Rite, in which the meshtw was used, the meshtw mirroring the constellation of Ursa Minor, a tool, linked to the stars. The Chanunpa, or Sacred Pipe, also mirroring the constellation of Ursa Minor, a tool, also linked to the stars, which sanctifies the human temple, the body, and carries our prayers up to Tunkashila, through the smoke of the Sacred Pipe mixture. The djed pillar perch on which the falcon rested and received instructions from the KA of the dead earth god in the primitive enclosure of the first temple of the First Time, mirrors the tsotsokpi of the Hopi altar on which perches the souls of the dead society members who have power over rain, just like the KA, communicating with the Falcon, had power over the primeval water. These "hits" or correlations point to the signature of the Shemsu Hor throughout the world. They had a message to give to mankind. It is up to us to listen.

The Sacred Pipe, the Meshtw, both having the form of Ursa Minor, the Tsotsokpi, the perch on the Hopi Altar where the souls of dead society members congregate, the Perch of the Djed, where the Ka communicated with the Falcon, Reeds, their importance in Hopi society and in Ancient Egypt, the First Mound on the Egyptian Temple representing the first land seen above water, the sand ridge on the Hopi Altar.

Builder Gods, Spider Woman, Maasaw and Kokopelli of the Hopi, the Egyptian Gods, Builder Gods, all survivors of a massive cataclysm which destroyed their homeland. They scattered all over the world building massive stone structures which had mathematical equations encoded within, a legacy left for future generations.

The Pharaoh Narmer, coming out of the old Kingdom considered himself a demi god, a descendant of the Builder Gods, and all Pharaohs of later period considered themselves having a divine link to those Builder Gods.

Egyptian Pharaohs had direct access to the secret language of hieroglyphics that still evades Egyptologists. Encoded language only reserved for those who were worthy.

CHAPTER THREE

OUTSIDE TIME

Coiled power.

"A star-goddess receives energy from the sun which enters her mouth. She passes it on to a serpent, the symbol of the earthly powers who are thus brought to life by a celestial energy. That which is above is as that which is below." (1)

Hamish Miller and Paul Broadhurst, in their book The Sun and the Serpent aptly describe the universal symbol of the serpent found in many cultures. Universal it is, this spiral power, from within us in the form of the DNA molecule to the outer reaches of the universe in the form of spiral galaxies.

In The Book of the Hopi, Frank Waters explains the deep meaning of the Snake-Antelope Ceremony. It is a "union of the two societies" in which the snake represents "a symbol of the mother earth from which all life is born." Furthermore, "it has a still deeper meaning. For as the bodies of man and the world are similar in structure, the deep bowels of the earth in which the snake makes its home are equate with the lowest of man's vibratory centers which controls his generative organs. The antelope, conversely, is associated with the highest center in man, for its horn is located at the top or crown of the head, the Kopavi, which in man is the place of coming in and going out of life, the "open door" through which he spiritually communicates with his Creator." (2). These polar opposites bring about the following: "Their mystic marriage is thus a fusing of man's dual forces within the body of their common ceremonial for the one constructive purpose of creation." (3).

29

This made absolute sense to me after I viewed the photographic plates of plaques and baskets in Helga Teiwes's book Hopi Basket Weaving. Teiwes states that the coiled pattern is the preferred pattern of plaques for the Niman (home) dance which she witnessed at Hotevilla in 1993. (4). After viewing the coiled plaques represented on the photographic plates, I realized the deep, secret meaning of the coiled, counter clockwise pattern of the plaques. Plaques are used to hold sacred cornmeal during ceremonies in the kivas. Usually, the patterns are simple; however, the important aspect of the plaque is how it is made: coiled counter clockwise, it represents life itself, the beginning of life, serpent power, and the completed end, followed clockwise, from the outside in, represents life enacted, the celestial run of a celestial program, to end at the center, and to start anew. I'm absolutely sure that the plaque's construction is a deliberate representation of the serpent power in action. Its use, to hold sacred cornmeal, further emphasizes its very sacred meaning to the Hopis during their ceremonials.

Further driving home the relationship between the Hopi plaques and serpent power is the taboo imposed on women not initiated in either the Lalkont or O'waqolt societies. Those not initiated would suffer a skin disease if they made plaques or baskets. (5). The skin is one of the most important organs the snake sheds periodically, symbolically representing the shedding of the old, the unwanted. The shedding of skin is one of the snake's unique trademark, and a disease of the skin would follow that link to the secret meaning of the coiled plaques and baskets of the Hopis.

The royal serpent symbol called the uraeus in Ancient Egypt was coiled, ready to strike, coiled power in action. The Hopis take great pains to ensure that the rattlesnakes are uncoiled in the kiva and during the Snake Dance; obviously because a coiled snake is dangerous and ready to strike. Ancient Egypt had a standing army which was, at its height, quite a formidable adversary. The Hopis are a peaceful, agricultural society (though aggression has flared up during their long history), so serpent power is about potential action transforming into rain through the Snake-Antelope Ceremony.

It is interesting to note that ceremonies involving snakes are found throughout the world, like India, for example. There might be a direct relationship with the labyrinth symbol, also found throughout the world and on rock carvings near Oraibi and Shipaulovi. (6). Perhaps these coiled labyrinths represent vortices at specific locations. The concentration of this energy was manifested by markers such as the stone rings found throughout England and France.

Going back to the very first quote in this chapter from the Sirius Connection by Murry Hope and comparing it to the following quote by Teiwes relating to her experience at the Lalkont dance will drive home the similarity of the star-goddess bringing down the energy from the sun to the serpent (in this case the Hopi woman/star-goddess bringing down the sun to the serpent/coiled plaque or basket) thus bringing life from celestial energy. "After the last dance, the women climbed to the roof of the kiva, took off their mantas, and stood for a short while among more mountains of plastic, paper, and aluminum household goods. Then the full moon rose behind the kiva, and the women, elevated as they were, were bathed in the last rays of the setting sun while we below them were obscured in the shade. It was a spectacular sight. Visual imprints of moments like this stay with us for the rest of our lives." (7).

The bringing down of celestial energy into the plaques imprint in the plaques that energy, and being on the roof of the kiva, a vortex point, focuses that energy even further into the sacred objects. The similarity with the Ancient Egyptian mural is striking, another "signature" of the Shemsu-Hor.

There is similarity between the Skidi priest observing the stars through a smoke hole of the earth lodge and the Hopi snake priest observing the Milky Way through the ladder opening with jars full of snakes resting on the kiva floor. The similarity rests with stellar knowledge shared by both, and as well with the Lakota and many other North American Indian nations. This connection between the earth and the sky is universal, and very much so with the Hopis whose snake symbol represents the earth. The kiva, sunken in the ground, oriented east-west rectangular fashion also connected with the earth, its ladder opening connecting to the stars, is a star gate, connecting man to a power outside time.

The kiva

Anasazi kivas used to be round. Hopi kivas today are rectangular, "the east-west axis formed by the path of the sun running through it lengthwise, and running cross wise the north-south axis of the earth, at whose end sit Poqanghoya and Palongawhoya who keep the planet rotating properly." (8).

Being below ground, the kiva represents Mother Earth, a womb, in which the priests conduct their ceremonies at its lower level, barefoot to indicate humility. (9). In all kivas, a hole, or sipapuni is found, representing man's emergence from the third world to the present fourth world. As indicated in chapter two, the Hopi altar is constructed in the kiva, tailored to the ceremony being performed.

Thus, in a nutshell, is what a kiva represents, a sacred place for the enactment of ceremony. The progression from round to rectangular kivas is not readily available though some theories are presented unsatisfactorily. (10). Voth spent a lot of time in Hopi kivas observing ceremonies. He even took an impressive amount of photographs of ongoing ceremonies and altars, a practice which would not be allowed today. Yet, the kiva is a lot more than what was photographed, measured and observed.

For example, let's start with an analogy. Let's say that having the capability, one transports a car body (right out of paint before anything is added to it) back in time to the period of Ramses the Second of Ancient Egypt. We place the car body in a village square early one morning and invisible, we observe people's reaction towards it. Many people would look at it, and puzzle over it. Perhaps some squatters would cart it off in the desert and use it as a dwelling. Perhaps soldiers would cart it off for Ramses II's inspection; scribes would dutifully record every word uttered by the high priests. But no one would know what it was though theories would abound by the hundreds.

Let's bring the stakes a little higher and transport a 1999 Gran Am GT unlocked, without keys to that village square, The analogy here is a kiva (the car body) with the altar and ceremonial accoutrements (the completed car). This time the Ancient Egyptians would recognize something such as wheels; however, being in park, and without an ignitions key, the vehicle would remain locked in park, therefore try as they could, the villagers would be unable to push the vehicle forward or backwards. Trial and error would reveal release points such as the hood and trunk release, the gas cover release and seat adjustment levers. Perhaps some really curious person would discover the fuse box. By the time the soldiers arrived some things would have disappeared like trunk tools, fuses, the spare tire. The soldiers and laborers would have a considerable harder time transporting the vehicle to the palace, but transport they would because Pharaoh demanded it.

At the palace, the vehicle would be intensely scrutinized for weeks. Learned Egyptians would correctly conclude that the vehicle was a form of transportation as evidenced by the seats, the wheels. Without proper tools however, disassembly would be impossible. People would spend months examining the engine without a clue as to its function. Possibly someone would discover how to siphon gas and after trial and error would discover it being flammable. Scribes would meticulously describe the vehicle slavishly and volumes would be written. Theories upon theories would be developed until a high priest would decree that the thing was evil resulting in its burial in a secret vault in the desert together with all its documentation.

My analogy, of course, is fantasy; but its purpose is to show several things. Much can be found related to the Hopi kivas, altars and ceremonies. One can find extremely detailed information throughout Voth's documentation and pictures. Many others have followed until the Hopis stopped the exploitation of their ceremonial ways. Yet, with all this information available, anthropologists are still in the dark relating to the how and why. Naively, anthropologists focus on the rain as a primary reason as to the why. Smugly, they point to the how by discussing the intricate aspects of Hopi ceremonialism. Yet, they are missing what the Ancient Egyptians would be missing in my analogy above: a key, an ignition key. Without the ignition key, the modern vehicle cannot be turned on, let alone, be taken out of park. Though its engine could be viewed, touched, studied, its purpose would be unfathomable to the Ancient Egyptians. So what might be viewed overtly and actually displayed by Hopis remains hidden by a strict adherence to cultural rules. Born Hopi and initiated into a society grants one an ignition key. But it's a key which cannot be shared with non- Hopis and with Hopis not initiated into the same society.

In Chapter Two, I had mentioned that without a "passport" we cannot hope to penetrate Hopi sacred knowledge. Even non-initiated Hopis don't possess a "passport" to Hopi society rituals. I did allude, however, to a peripheral hint to this sacred knowledge. This knowledge is about stars, time, and space.

Each time I visited Anasazi kivas and viewed photographs of Hopi kivas the word portal came to mind; a portal to other worlds, dimensions.

Earlier I had mentioned that the Hopi kiva is rectangular in shape. This is quite unusual because sacred spaces throughout the world are circular. Fred Alan Wolf in his book The Eagle's Quest mentions that the circle is a universal symbol. Mr Wolf noted that the circle is found in every shamanic tribe on earth and that the circle is closer to quantum physics than Newtonian physics. (11). So why is the Hopi kiva rectangular?

Fred Alan Wolf develops a fascinating background relating to time travel and shamanism in his chapter titled Time Traveling and Visions of Past and Future (12). It seems that shamans possess a knowledge which taps into physics relating to the very source which holds this universe together.

When I was working as an Indian Health Service Nurse at Tuba City, Arizona, work was being done to bury the uranium mine there with heavy basaltic rock. The burial was necessary because of the nature of the uranium ore. Tuba City was a source for uranium for the Manhattan Project during World War II. The uranium ore at Tuba City is hot, and leaching of yellow uranium oxide can be found in the desert, exposed. The place, including Black Mesa is uranium rich.

Interestingly, besides Black Mesa, the Rosebud Lakota Reservation is also uranium rich. Fred Allan Wolf states the following:

"…a lot of sacred sites are close to uranium and other mineral deposits. In fact, that's what a lot of land-rights issues of the Australian aborigines and American Indians are still about-they have sacred sites on areas the governments want to mine for their uranium deposits." (13). Earlier in the book Wolf comments on the interesting relationship between radioactivity and shamanism: "I began to speculate that there was a specific connection between shamanic consciousness and radiation discovered around sacred sites-where the "world-crack" was very thin. In fact it was, probably, radiation that induced shamanic visions. I had no idea how that radiation made shamans vibrationally attuned to the sacred grounds of their birthplaces. Perhaps it had something to do with the amount of radioactive carbon or other elements absorbed by the human system being slightly different in different countries. The shaman born of a particular land, ate of that land, and thereby contained a similar amount of radioactive carbon in his system. This would render her or him sensitive to place. Would shamans continue to go to places where these extraordinary events would occur?" (14).

The "world-crack" Wolf is referring to is the portal between worlds, possibly within our universe and also possibly with parallel universes. So it is not surprising to find spiritual centers and structures like kivas in close proximity to very high concentrations of uranium ore. And where uranium is found, gold is not too far away.

Going back to the rectangular Hopi kiva, its shape, a departure from a circle, tells me that energy, generated from ceremony, is focused differently. If one recalls the shape of the Ark of the Covenant, an acacia box gold plated inside and out which became live with power when the tablets were placed within, one could draw an analogy with the Hopi kiva, especially when one observes the objects of the first field of the Hopi altar which contains an altar frame and boards. These flat boards have cloud and lightning symbols either painted or carved. Of course we don't see overtly gold on the inner and out walls of the kiva; and we don't see overtly an energy source, a radioactive source which is suspected to be within the Ark of the Covenant (15) in the Hopi kiva. But I began to suspect, with the shape of the Hopi kiva, a deliberate intent to focus the energy which would have the effect of an echo, an amplification effect of the confined energy generated through ritual. The flat clay and stone objects, and flat boards remind me of the tabots, also flat boards, found in Ethiopian churches which represent replicas of the tablets found in the Ark of the Covenant. Flat, rectangular structures, in a rectangular kiva, perhaps radioactive due to the uranium in the clay or paint with, perhaps, gold within the walls of the kiva would literally transform the Hopi kiva into an Ark where energy is amplified to an extreme fashion through ritual based on the kiva's shape.

All of this is speculation on my part. Yet, I feel that I'm not far from the reason as to why the Hopi kiva is rectangular. A shape is not changed without a reason. And the reason, in this case, is energy, how energy is to be used and focused. This I'm absolutely convinced of. As to examining a kiva in detail today would be out of the question. However, many of the boards and other ceremonial objects are disposed of at different shrines. Possibly a Geiger counter reading of these objects would either confirm or rule out radioactivity. However, even if ruled out, going back to what Wolf stated, ceremonial sites are usually found in close proximity of uranium ore. This fits the case with the Hopis as well as with the Navajo and Lakota. Their settling near such a source was not by accident. It was intentional because the Hopi ancestors knew that the veil between worlds was thin and that even today the Hopis know this and still perform their ceremonies based on that knowledge.

So amidst all this radioactivity, why aren't the Hopis sick? How come one finds extreme longevity and good health amidst the Hopi elders? The reason might stem from how the energy is used. It used wrong, it could seriously hurt. It might even kill. If the energy is used properly within rules established by the Creator, then no harm will occur. This is precisely why the Hopis have kept their ceremonies secret. The portals they open within the kivas allow energies to flow in that are so powerful that those without the proper knowledge and training would either be seriously hurt or killed, or cause irreversible harm to the world.

This coiled power, this serpent power is scattered throughout the globe at various sacred sites. This power is usually associated with uranium ore and perhaps gold. It was known by the Ancient Egyptians and today, is known and applied through ceremonies and symbolic objects such as the coiled plaques by the Hopis. This shared, sacred physics can only point to a shared knowledge disseminated by teachers a long long time ago. This sacred physics points to a knowledge of Creational energy. But this energy can only be utilized through balance and harmony. Any other way will result in chaotic energy caused by uncontrolled release. Perhaps this has already occurred when the first atomic bomb was detonated. It might have caused a severe ripple through space and time which might have accounted for a rash of UFOs over nuclear sites in 1947. An interdimensional visit? As Col. Phillip J. Corso (Ret) states in his book The Day after Roswell "Maybe the Roswell crash, which helped us develop the technological basis for weapons systems to protect our planet from the EBEs, was also a mechanism for successfully implanting a completely alien nonhumanoid life-form that survives from host to host like a virus, a digital Ebola that we humans will carry to another planet someday. Or what if an enemy wanted to implant the perfect spying or sabotage mechanism into a culture? Then the implementation of the microchip-based circuit into our technology by the EBEs would be a perfect method. Was it implanted as sabotage or as something akin to the gift of fire? Maybe the Roswell crash in 1947 was an event waiting to happen, like poisoned fruit dropping from the tree into a playground. Once bitten, the poison takes effect." (16).

Did we unintentionally open a portal with the first atomic bomb? And by doing so, did we take a bite from the poisoned apple?

I was in Las Vegas Nevada for several weeks doing research regarding the Janet Airlines which takes workers to and from Area 51. Many other areas of interest were examined, based on Col Corso's book. It was also a time period for the Photo Marketing International photo convention in Las Vegas which I studied with great interest as well. Many strange things happened during that trip but the strangest occurred at a McDonald's across the street from the Mandalay Bay hotel. I was having a cup of coffee after a photo shoot of the Janet Airline terminal down the street. A woman walked in and went to the counter. She had multiple badges one would wear to get access to a business, or a place together with ID. All were carefully turned to the blank side. As she waited for her order, I saw her drill me with her eyes-I will never forget that face, it was pale, triangular in shape, with incredibly intense eyes. My mind was suddenly overwhelmed by a message, "Be careful. Do not approach. Do not follow." I felt rooted in place as she got her order and added some things from the condiment section, then left. I ripped myself from my seat, I felt wooden, and had difficulty getting going but I did and exited McDonald's. I looked left and right but did not see the woman. Instead, I saw two men, with military haircuts, well built just hanging around at the curb. I got the feeling they noticed me just by their careful nonchalance of avoiding eye contact. I proceeded to the street to cross, watching obliquely if any movement was made by the two men.

Half way across the street towards the Mandalay Bay the two men were on the move one going down the street the other following. By the time I reached the sidewalk, the other guy was also crossing the street.

I knew the layout of the Mandalay Bay hotel and its gardens, and access points to the gardens which I took, and under cover of vegetation ran towards the entrance. As I got to the entrance I saw the two men walking very fast towards me but I had created a significant distance between them.

I immediately went in and knew that a restaurant was close by so I ducked into it and went to the rear near some windows and got a table blocked by a large group of people. I peeked at the entrance and soon saw the men racing into the hotel where they split one going one way the other another way.

I decided to leave and went out and peeked around a corner and saw one of the men walking very fast his head on a swivel at some distance.

I melted out through the gardens again and was fortunate in hailing a taxi getting out of the area as fast as possible, going back to the Photo convention.

I felt it was good Tradecraft, and my thoughts went back to the mysterious woman at McDonald's. I especially thought about her intense eyes, and the overwhelming message I got in my mind. What was she? Where did she work? The one thought that came to me was that she was a hybrid, an alien, but in human form, walking among us, hidden in plain sight. Working for our government. Who were the two military types? Why did they follow me?

As a researcher, photographer, I notice small details. I have a very developed situational awareness. My brain has a built in radar which warns me of unusual behavior, different things and people that just don't fit. When triggered, I can't shake it off. My experience at the McDonald's and at the Mandalay Bay hotel were real.

Did I have an alien contact at the McDonald's? Yes, I believe so. Do I believe the two military types were shadowing the woman? Yes, I believe so. Was the woman's warning real? Yes, it was. How did she know about me? I felt totally "searched" when that woman drilled me with her eyes-she knew in an instant everything about me. She had incredible situational awareness and locked onto to me. Like a radar, but a lot better than mine. She knew I would know. She knew I would recognize her. Thus the warning. Do not approach. Don't even acknowledge me. I know you know. For your safety do not follow.

We meet people from other cultures and the contacts makes us excited, learning from them, interacting with them. This was totally different. This was at another unexperienced level. The experience was outwordly.

To this day I believe I had an alien contact. In Las Vegas. In

plain sight. By someone who is "in" our government system, working, in plain sight.

Who likes McDonald's.

CHAPTER FOUR

QUEST FOR INNOCENCE

Pre-Flight.

Just as a helicopter pilot must go thru a pre-flight checklist prior to takeoff, a candidate must also go through a series of steps in order to become initiated to a mystery or secret society. This process requires a breaking down, a reduction. This deprogramming is vital before the candidate clears the final step of initiation, death itself.

It appears that this reduction brings the candidate close to a state which is incompatible with the established social programming. This reduction might even involve the very code of life, DNA.

Take, for example, children.

Children are pure and are closer to the source of Creation than, let's say, adults. Children are still, however, under the spell of cellular programming which is very much influenced by social triggers. I believe that we have very sensitive "set switches" in our DNA which either close or open in response to these social triggers. These "set switches" might have been planted in order for us to forget our roots.

Contrary to standard texts, the Gnostics believed that the serpent was beneficial to mankind, bringing about a spiritual awakening. (1). The Gnostics considered the Old Testament Jehovah "as a dark force, indeed as the 'world rulers of darkness' an 'Archon' whose purpose was to keep mankind chained for eternity in spiritual ignorance." (2).

Michael Harner, through a vision induced by the hallucinogenic ayahuasca describes, in The Way of the Shaman how dragon like creatures hid within all creatures of the earth, including man, in order to disguise themselves and escape from an enemy in deep space. (3). The Archangel Michael depicted as battling a dragon can be seen on innumerable stained glass windows throughout churches and cathedrals in Europe. This despised dragon, however, might be what Harner depicts in retrospect in his footnote as closely resembling DNA, the very program of life that the dragon creatures introduced on earth and which the Archons have desperately attempted to eradicate or perhaps change by manipulation.

To change the very code of life, however, is perhaps an attempt to darken our spiritual awareness. Perhaps we have modern Archons today, here on earth, working on the human DNA with that very intent.

The Hopi Snake Society performs a cultural deprogramming by exposing young children to snakes during the washing of the snakes in the kiva. Voth describes this in The Oraibi Summer Snake Ceremony. There is no reason not to believe that the exact thing is happening today in other snake kivas. This description, I believe, is a method, by the Snake Society, to reverse the "set switches" permanently within the children's DNA. These children, helping the Snake Society priests will in turn become future snake priests for the Snake Society.

Voth describes the children's role as follows:

"But return we now to the bathing of the snakes. One has followed the other until all have gone through the two baths and been placed on the sand field. When the snakes see that they cannot escape they finally pile up in a corner on the floor and on the banquette (see PL. 195), enjoying the sunshine that falls on those places through the hatchway just at that time. Occasionally, one tries to escape, especially the racers, but usually one or two boys, who are left in charge, can manage them. When the washing is complete, the three men who handled the snakes carefully wash their hands and then the chief priest and one or two others usually utter a brief prayer, whereupon all seat themselves around the fireplace and smoke, exchanging terms of relationship. The snakes are left in charge of one or two of the small boys. In 1896 little Hoveima, who was then a lad of about ten years, herded or watched them alone (see A, PL. 195), though they kept him very busy when the other men had withdrawn." (4).

According to Voth, this very solemn ceremony was witnessed by very few anthropologists. The reason for washing the snakes was not given to him.

Yet it seems to me that a partial reason lies with a desensitizing process for both the adults and children. Most importantly, for the children, their fear towards the snakes is forever eradicated by their close proximity with them. Furthermore, Voth observed the children handling and playing with the snakes, rattlesnakes included, as casually as if they were handling kittens.

It's all in the handling of the snakes:

Voth suggested the following relating to this procedure: (4) "The repeated handling of the snakes undoubtedly makes them more or less gentle. There is no question but what the priests are more afraid of the snakes when they first capture them later. One of them, in explaining to me the details of the snake hunt, emphasized the fact that they at once commence to "tame" them by careful handling and by slowly stroking them, and when I asked him why so very seldom one was bitten by any snake, he said he would only explain it by careful handling of the snakes. He said they never hurt the snakes and hence the latter became used to them and were not afraid of them. He compared the case with that of a wild pony, which, when first caught, would "kick, bite, and jump," but when repeatedly and carefully handled would become gentle; The snakes, being often touched by the point of the snake whips, become used to seeing objects over themselves and to being touched by them, and hence do not find it so strange when a hand reaches towards them. It must be added, however, that if this point explains anything, it does so to a limited extent only, as snakes are brought in even up to the last days, which form the very nature of the case have been handled but very little; The principle explanation, therefore, does not, I believe, lie in the frequency of the handling, but rather the manner in which it is done. I have again and again seen the snakes picked up in the kivas and on the plazzas, put into and taken out of jars, jugs, and bags, not only in Oraibi, but in all the villages, by the old experienced priests as well as by the novices, but only very seldom have I seen one reach after or grasp a reptile with a quick, jerking, hesitating movement of the hand, and even on those few occasions the snakes were generally trying to get away, at least they were not in a proper position to strike when taken. Under ordinary circumstances the movement of the hand, in trying to take a snake is slow and gentle, but sure and unhesitating. I saw old, half-blind Nuvakwahu reach towards several snakes, that with heads raised and drawn back, were watching the approaching hand, and that probably would have struck, since they were at least partially coiled, had they noticed the least twitching or jerking of the hand. Never, at any time, have I seen even the most experienced member of the Fraternity try to take a snake when the reptile was entirely coiled up. They seem to be convinced, and in fact have told me, that a rattlesnake does not strike unless entirely coiled up or at least nearly so. If a snake does coil up it is invariably first induced to uncoil by waving the snake whip over it." (5).

Developing trust to regain lost innocence…with serpent power.

Let's pause for a moment and reflect.

The only thing man can hope to do with DNA is splice, reattach and manipulate its structure.

Man cannot make DNA out of nothing.

So if the Dragons brought DNA to earth…according to Harner…

Then the Dragon: is it…

By observing the universe and all its coiled representations…

Perhaps the representations of a Creator of this universe…

And the opposition, man-like, and evil, forever attempting to destroy serpent representations…

Especially in man…

Perhaps the very evil cleverly hidden within some organized religions…

Are the Archons themselves, jealous and forever denouncing the Dragon as the supreme evil entity of all time.

"A star-goddess receives energy from the sun which enters her mouth. She passes it on to a serpent, the symbol of the earthly powers who are brought to life by a celestial energy. That which is above is as that which is below." (6)

Instead of being represented as an enemy, the serpent is represented as a link between the creational energy above and earthly powers below. It's also within all life on earth. It is inescapable, and to eradicate it would mean eradicating spiritual power and life.

"Perhaps the representations of a Creator of this universe…"

Fred Allan Wolf in his book Parallel Universes explores the theories of parallel universes to our own. The scenarios he presents are dizzying and mind twisting. Yet, possibly, as Wolf mentions in his book The Eagle's

Quest, "world-cracks" occur in areas of high uranium concentrations; be it that the "world-cracks" are doorways, star gates from this serpentine universe to other parallel universes accessed through the Hopi kivas. This universe, therefore, might be similar yet different from parallel universes to our own.

We have, so far, travelled to the Hopi lands, explored their altars, and linked some of their ceremonial practices to Ancient Egypt. A stellar relationship began to emerge, linking not only the Ancient Egyptians and the Hopis but also to the Skidi Pawnee and the Lakota. A shamanic physics began to reveal itself by Fred Allan Wolf's observation that shamans are drawn to certain sites such as those with high concentrations of uranium. Harner's vision, and the universal theme of snake power and world vortices point to a knowledge far beyond coincidence. Such sacred knowledge linking so many cultures indicate a force through time which has fought to keep the spiritual flame lit within mankind by cleverly seeding this information through different media. The hope was to saturate this information throughout the world like lighthouses, continuously sending beacons of light in a world darkened by forces which want the lights extinguished.

The soul, as was mentioned earlier, is perpetually in danger of losing its connection to the Divine Light. But what is the soul? Where is its connection to the material body? And how does it avoid the pitfalls the Ancient Egyptians feared and who went to great lengths to chart a navigational map to its hoped destination? And how did the Hopi ancestors know that a charted passage was necessary to the soul's successful course?

Parallel universes and DNA seen very much like two subjects which have absolutely nothing in common. Yet as these themes are developed in the next chapters, a deeper understanding of the soul will evolve as it relates to what was discussed relating to the Hopi kiva and the Egyptian first time.

In Endnote 11 Chapter 2, netted gourd vessels are used by two priestesses who took them to the springs. One might say that a netted gourd would be necessary in order to transport water. It seems like a very reasonable tool. The coiled plaques too seem to be reasonable tools to transport sacred cornmeal into the kivas. However, as it was mentioned earlier, a deeper significance was attributed to the coiled plaques, directly linking them to serpent power.

So what is so special with the netted gourd vessel?

Just like the coiled plaques, an object such as a net should be examined carefully in order to see beyond its everyday function. Its utilitarian function camouflages sacred meaning. The beauty of the item is that it can be displayed in public without revealing sacred knowledge. Yet in the net lies the keys to high order physics which is stellar in nature with a twist: interdimensional travel.

Perhaps our universe is visited by interdimensional travelers. Perhaps the 'Archons' themselves are from another dimension who have exerted their power on "our turf". How those doorways are opened requires extreme spiritual maturity; one might not know what might come through the door.

CHAPTER FIVE

THE NET

On the girdle-wall of the Temple of Edfu in Egypt a net is portrayed. The scene represents ""The capture of the enemies of the god". Who are symbolized by waterfowl, certain fishes and gazelles, together with some human captives." (1). The net appears to be on a sort of bark, held secure by a rope which weaves through the middle of the net. At the very top can be seen birds, some with wings extended, others at rest, each on top of a bulrush; what is striking is the predominance of birds at the top of the net. Clearly, those birds are not caught by the net. They are free to fly away unhindered.

Are we part of the creatures caught on the net, waiting for our turn to transcend our captive state and be free like the birds depicted above?

Then, while reading Fred Allan Wolf's Parallel Universes, I came across a figure on page 167 titled "The infinite patchwork of parallel universes in a spinning black hole found by Roy Kerr." (2). The figure looks strangely like the net of the Edfu Temple, especially when comparing the rope depicted above with the singularities bisecting Kerr's "net".

Wolf explains that "Kerr's solution was marked as one of the most important developments in theoretical astrophysics of the mid-twentieth century. The factor we want to examine is that Kerr's equations indicated the existence of an infinite number of parallel universes, all connected with the spin of the hole."

"Because the hole is spinning, there are two event horizons, an outer and an inner. A spacetime voyager can now safely pass from our universe into any other parallel universe with the exception of one parallel universe. Because of the structure of the honeycomb map constructed by Kerr, it is possible to travel to all other universes except one without ever moving faster than the speed of light. The exceptional parallel universe is the one adjacent to our own. To reach it, you must exceed the speed of light, which is not possible." (3).

My goal is to show relationships between cultures, not describe in detail the theories of space and time. Fred Allan Wolf's book splendidly explains horrendously complex theories in a way easily understood by the layman. Stephen Hawkins also brilliantly explains the theories of space and time, black holes and other universes in his book A brief History of Time. Also absent are the complex equations which can be found in an earlier Hawkins book titled The large scale structure of space-time. (4).

But Wolf's quote above describes the mathematical result which translates into a "honeycomb map" which resembles very much the Edfu net especially when the singularities are included, resembling the rope holding the net upright on the strange bark like construction of the Edfu mural.

Singularities, according to Wolf, "are regions of spacetime where gigantic distortions, possibly even rips in the fabric of spacetime, appear. At a singularity, all physical quantities take on infinite values. These singularities exist at the centers of objects called black holes. In these black holes, space and time become highly stretched. Time intervals stretch so much that light slows down to zero speed as it approaches one. In other words, light stops, moving at the center of a black hole, and the laws of physics go crazy. In the vincinity of these distortions there are gateways to other universes. The first to discover one of these gateways was Einstein and Nathan Rosen. It is now even called the Einstein-Rosen bridge, and it connects two different parallel universes." (5).

Then I discovered other diagrams in the Sefer Yetzirah, The Book of Creation by Aryeh Kaplan. Notable, on the cover, is represented "The paths defined by the Gra, as they appear in Warsaw, 1884 edition. (p. 26b of Part Two). (6).

Now if you tilt this diagram on its side you will notice a similarity with the net of Edfu and Kerr's honeycomb map. And bisecting the three diamonds can be seen a line which strangely resembles the rope bisecting the Edfu map and the singularities of the Kerr map. (see diagrams 1-3).

Dr Paul Brunton states, in his book A search in Secret Egypt, that Moses was an Adept, initiated to the innermost secrets of Ancient Egypt's occult knowledge. (7). The original Pentateuch document, according to Brunton, was written by Moses himself in Egyptian hieroglyphs. (8). The code of the sacred hieroglyphic text, unfortunately, was not translated adequately, so the meaning became more and more obscure as time went by.

Moses as an Egyptian High Priest, a Hierophant, is no fantasy; in his youth, he was taught and initiated because he belonged to the royal family. This is one aspect which was very quickly forgotten by Hebrew scholars. So the information he brought forth in the desert later on in life was not from a divine origin; it was from his vast accumulated knowledge of Ancient Egypt's occult science which contained the very secrets of the universe.

So going back to Kaplan's book: figure 3 on page 28 shows different arrays of the 32 paths. May it be, perhaps, that the 32 paths represent an interdimensional map; because further, on page 185, the Sefer Yetzirah describes the "Seven Universes", or "the Seven Chambers in the Universe of Beriyah." Does this suggest that we are part of a seven universe array within an endless chain of parallel universes?

Murry Hope suggests that the net had something to do with time in her book The Sirius Connection. (9). Budge connects Thoth with the net: "It is quite clear that in the Egyptian legend the god Thoth was supposed to have some connection with the newt of Ra, and it is equally clear that in his temple, which was called the Temple of the Net, the emblem of a net, or perhaps even a net itself, was venerated." (10).

If one examines carefully the obscure prayer relating to the net in the Book of the Dead (Chapter cliii.) the following drops out as significant: "I go a-fishing with cordage of the 'uniter of the earth' (Horus?), and of him that maketh a way through the earth." Further on, "the rope..." "which had a frame which reached unto heaven, and weighted parts that rested upon the earth>" (11). Again, we see the symbol of a rope, a uniter making a way through the earth with a rope, a frame, with weights, which rest on the earth...singularities? Access points on the earth to other dimensions? What is the frame? Is it one of the frames, one of the squares of the net? Is the frame our universe? Is it a warning to follow a strict passage in order to get to a desired destination?

Perhaps the net at Edfu is like the X found on the proverbial treasure map. The Ancient Egyptians did not engrave symbols at random; there was a purpose. Is the net mural at Edfu a marker for something very significant? Does it mark a spot where there is a "world-crack"? Is it an access point to another dimension? Is the Edfu net mural a marker for something which has not been discovered yet?

If we go back to the Hopi medicine altar, you may recall that water plays an important role in its construction. The medicine altar ritual "transforms the medicine altar itself into a surrogate Sipaapuni. In this manner, the altar and its kiva becomes a ritualized world center." (12). Acting as a focal point, "the medicine bowl, like its Sipaapuni counterpart, is a gateway through which the denizens of the spirit world can pass into the dimensions of physical reality." (13). Geertz describes the medicine bowl as a "projector"; so he is not too far in describing the medicine altar, the third field of the main altar, as a focal point, a lens, for an interdimensional event during Hopi ceremonialism.

Earlier, in chapter two, a netted gourd vessel was mentioned under endnote 11 together with other objects the priestess took with them to the springs. It is interesting to note that women went to the spring to gather water.

In the "net" prayer earlier, the fishers "go round about in the chambers of the waters". (14). Interestingly, one finds water associated with chambers in the Sefer Yetzirah: from verse 1:12: "as it is written…" Kaplan writes: "The complete verse is. "He lays the beams of His upper chambers with water…He makes breaths His angels, His ministers of flaming fire." God's "upper chambers" are the spiritual universes, while His lower chamber is the physical world. The ceiling beams of His upper chambers are said to me made of water. This refers to the level above Beriyah, which is Atzilut. In Atzilut, Chakhmah is dominant, and Chakhmah is represented by water." (15). Earlier, Kaplan states that "According to the philosophers, Water represents the primeval matter, while fire represents the primitive aether. (223-Kuzar i4:25 (58)." (16).

One must understand that water, as mentioned in the Sefer Yetzirah does not represent physical water; it represents something entirely different. (17). Does it represent some type of energy? Chakhmah being part of the 32 paths: then what does the 32 paths represent? If the 32 paths, as defined by the Ari and the Gra, are tilted on one side, don't they appear like the Edfu net; furthermore, what are the connections between the so called spheres? Interdimensional paths?

Water, being a sacred substance and carried in a netted gourd by the two Hopi priestesses from the springs is poured at each cardinal direction into the medicine bowl. Activated by the priestesses at the springs with an eagle bone whistle and again, in the kiva, after the third song, the water thus becomes empowered together with all the ceremonial tasks as outlined in endnote 11. The medicine bowl then transforms into a portal, and the deceased society members are given access to the kiva and take their places on the tsotsokpis. The net around the water gourds represent in a symbolic way to me the same interdimensional nets above linking all to a common knowledge from deep antiquity. It is high level physics camouflaged within spiritual ritual.

Interdimensional travel might seem impossible in a physical sense; yet who knows? Some unexplained disappearances might explain interdimensional slips. A key, however, would be important in order to insure a return trip to our universe. The soul, however, seems to travel to other dimensions without any problems as evidenced by the preparations in the Hopi kiva. Those preparations line up the combinations necessary in order to open a portal. However, even if one copied verbatim one of the rituals outlined by Voth, nothing would happen. The ignition key is missing. The ignition key would be invisible to the non- initiates. Careful, meticulous observation would not be enough.

A good analogy would be the Edfu net mural. To the non-initiate, the Edfu net is just a net on which are caught various animals and people. On closer analysis, however, just like I outlined above, the Edfu net takes on a different meaning. And yet, even after cracking the mystery in a small way, the larger part of the mystery remains. Why was the mural placed in the Edfu temple? What else is buried there? And even is we found "something" would we recognize its purpose?

Caught on the Edfu net are perhaps the souls caught in this dimension, unable to progress further. Free, progressed souls, as represented by the birds at the very top might be the goal we are all striving for on this plane. But what is the soul, and what would keep the soul caught on the physical, dimensional net?

According to Buddhists, we accumulate a karmic bank account based on what we do and don't do in this physical lifetime. The stronger our attachments, the harder it is to separate from this physical reality.

These attachments appear to be magnetic in character; they attach to something within us. So we build attachments to this physical realm, and we continuously loop back into it through innumerable incarnations.

This dimensional testing ground is what the Edfu net represents. So what is it inside us which pulls us back to our attachments?

The Ancient Egyptians break down the soul as the BA and the KA. Isha Schwaller De Lubiscz explains the BA and KA quite well:

"In relation to the KA, BA is the animating spirit. In relation to BA, KA is the individualization of consciousness in the relatively subtle or gross states of being; it enables the animating spirit to become fixed."

"Ba carries the vital breath; its characteristic in non-fixity. BA always needs something to support it. KA is a principle of fixity and fixation-attraction. It is the power capable of attracting, fixing, and transforming the vital animating principle, BA. The word beka which expresses impregnation and fecundation of the female ovum, shows the association of these two elements necessary for a conception-an incarnation of the specific and essential Ka, given in the seed and animated by the vital breath of *b*." (18)

What is hinted here is that the soul is magnetically attracted to this physical reality by a part of it, the KA. Where does it reside?

Earlier, I mentioned that everything we do and don't do is being recorded, creating a karmic bank account. I believe that the biological tape recorder is within our DNA. This link pulls us back into the net if our attachments are too strong, or if we have a karmic debt to pay off. This magnetic link is so strong that it might follow family lines for centuries. And the cycle of physical life continues until we get it right. Then we can be free like the birds depicted above the Edfu net.

Have I gone crackers suggesting that the DNA molecule could be the seat for the soul? I'm suggesting a hypothesis, loaded with tantalizing clues. It's a radical, different idea, yet, I don't believe it to be too far from the truth. In order to continue on, however, the idea requires an open mind.

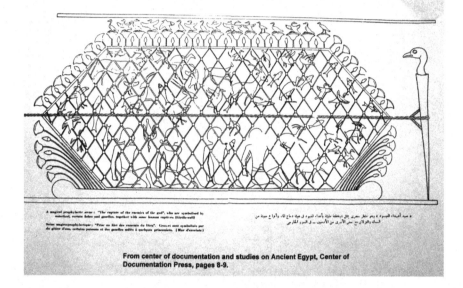

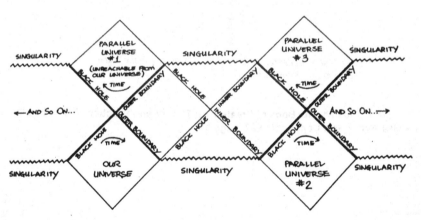

THE INFINITE PATCHWORK OF PARALLEL UNIVERSES
IN A SPINNING BLACK HOLE FOUND BY ROY KERR

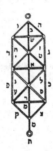

Figure 6. The paths defined by the Gra, as they appear in the Warsaw.
1884 edition. (p. 26b of Part Two).

CHAPTER SIX

A COSMIC RADIO

Embalmed for Eternity.

""The soul to heaven, the body to earth;" 1" (1).

On the surface, this sentence appears simple and straight forward. Upon death, the soul leaves the body behind including all other earthly possessions. So there is no need to concern oneself with the body; or should there be?

Budge states that "When we think of the sublime character of the life in heaven with the gods, it is hard to understand why the Egyptians took such pains to preserve the physical body from decay. No Egyptian who believed his Scriptures ever expected that his corruptible body would ascend into heaven and live with the gods, for they declare in no uncertain manner that is remains upon the earth whilst the soul dwells in heaven." (2).

Body preservation is not just found in Egypt. It shares a world -wide practice from the bogs of England, to the mountains of Peru; and from the Arctic wilderness to the sands of Mongolia. The practice is found everywhere, yet the question remains as to why.

The Ancient Egyptians used deliberate embalming methods which varied slightly through the centuries. These methods differed from other cultures which used the environment, such as intense cold, or tannin rich bogs; preservation was accomplished naturally. All share, however, a common desire to preserve the dead from decay. There seems to have been a heavy investiture in the preservation of the dead worldwide.

The Ancient Egyptian embalming practices can be broken down into three areas: 1-the technical, mechanical aspect of embalming; 2-the religious aspect which includes all of the ceremonies, spells and formulas; and 3-the spiritual aspects which tie in with the ceremonies, but deals directly with Ancient Egyptian cosmology and the soul.

These three areas gravitate around the Osirian Mysteries which reach into deep antiquity.

Osiris is directly related to life and resurrection. There is an emphasis, in the Osirian legend, on the scattering of Osiris's 14 or 16 body parts by Set. These body parts were later recovered by Osiris's sister and wife Isis who built a tomb at each site where a body part was found and buried. A cult grew out of these sacred sites where sanctuaries were built and became the focus of elaborate ceremonies during the month of Khoiak (3). Budge states that "various sanctuaries are described, and detailed instructions are given for the making of the funeral chest, and of the model of the god which was to be buried in the coffin, and of the incense, and of the amulets, and of the fourteen divine members, and of all the materials, etc., which were employed in the ceremonies." (4). Budge describes a strange object called the Hennu Boat which carried a coffer which contained "the body of the dead Sun-god Af, or of Osiris, and it rested upon a framework or sledge which was provided with runners. On the great day of the festival of Seker which was celebrated in many places throughout Egypt, the ceremony of placing the Seker boat upon its sledge was performed at sunrise, at the moment when the rays of the sun were beginning to spread themselves over the earth. The whole ceremony was under the direction of the high priest of Memphis, whose official title was "Ur kherp hem,""""i.e., great chief of the hammer"; this official was expected to lift the Seker Boat upon its sledge, and to march at the head of the procession of priests which drew the loaded sledge round the sanctuary. By this action the revolution of the sun and other celestial bodies was symbolized, but no texts explaining the symbolism have come down to us." (5).

The symbolic body of Osiris, real or not, transformed, through legend, into the cult of embalming in Ancient Egypt. According to legend, Osiris's body was incorruptible; however, through the help of Thoth, Osiris was embalmed and is frequently depicted as a mummy wearing a White Crown and a menat (hanging from the back of his neck." (6).

There seems to be an obsession on the part of the Ancient Egyptians to preserve the body for eternity. The puzzle which presents itself is that if the soul of the dead king went forward to Orion and became a star (according to the Pyramid Texts) then why would the body be so important here on earth. The answer may lie in part with the Ancient Egyptian soul concept called the KA.

The KA

"Definitive rebirth or resurrection is absolute complementation. BA is the volatile, the subtile, and KA is the energetic fixity which is the magnet for BA. The text says that the BA must recover its KA." (7).

The text R.A. Schwaller De Lubicz referes to is the Pyramid Text 578-579 which reads: "Your son Horus has smitten him" (Seth). "he has wrested his Eye from him and has given it to you; you have a soul by means of it, you have power by means of it at the head of the spirits." (8).

De Lubicz explains that "The subtle part which separates from the individual at death naturally seeks its supporting point in order to take form again, but if it has retained a regret or a violent desire, this will cause it to seek any substance whatsoever, a psychic in particular, borrowed from a living being, in order to return to a ghostlike shadow-existence. Real personal reincarnation can only be achieved by the reunion of the BA with its KA (17) (this pertains to the BA as animating spirit and to the Osirian KA called "KA of transformation") as the texts confirm." (9).

It appears that our physical desires and unfinished business in the physical realm gets us caught again and again on the net. Norman Mailer, in his earthy novel Ancient Evenings, describes the four lives of an Ancient Egyptian called Menenhetet. I found the novel depressing in its rendition of physical pain, love, war, in essence, all of what one feels during a lifetime, in this case four lifetimes which ends in physical death each time. Perhaps Norman Mailer's skilled writing enabled me, the reader, to feel that emotion. Yet, with all of its pain, we choose the net, and on the anvil of physical life we are hammered with the hammer of experience. The net is the arena of experience, the testing ground of the soul; and if we choose not to learn, the net is always there to catch us after we die to start anew; and once again we strive for the freedom of the birds above the net. Perhaps this one lifetime, we say. One must remember, however, what Buddha answered to the man who asked how many lifetimes he would have to reincarnate; the Buddha replied as many times as there were leaves on the very large tree under which they were sitting. That's a lot of leaves.

So what makes us so damn stubborn?

The Buddhist would respond that it's our attachments to the physical plane which keeps us fixed here and that one should practice meditation towards the goal of un-attachment. We must, however, contend with the KA which is "expressed by the word for the animal skin, meska product of the KA. The KA in question is that the earthly animal-man, the instinctive-emotional being who suffers the influence of the animal KAs of the viscera. It is to him that funeral offerings are made, to appease appetites that survive the animal body a longer or shorter time, depending on man's spiritual condition." (10). Further on, Isha Schwaller De Lubicz states that "as soon as the KA has taken flesh it becomes a personal urge, a will to live, that becomes the Me, inek. Nek, primitive blind force of human animality, quite without higher sensibility, is the principle of egoism; and this, growing with the child, crystallizes the KA's tendencies to its own advantage, to affirm its existence and assure its continuity. This inek, this Me, that seems to be the true individual, is in fact nothing but a reflection of KA and the individual's KAs." (11).

The KA, being the magnetic link to our physicality, pulls us into the net if we have not progressed spiritually. The KA being magnetic, has a powerful tie with the body. The Ancient Egyptians knew this, and knew that the body, being the testing tool within the realm of the net, was the link, the seat of the KA.

The BA, which goes forward in the spirit realm to get "debriefed" must keep communication line open with the KA. The reason for this is that in all probability, the Ba will have to come back and reincarnate. Possibly this explains why the Ancient Egyptians felt that it was important to die within one's homeland. (12).

Isha Schwaller De Lubicz summarizes quite well the Ancient Egyptian soul concept in her book Her-Bak:

"like animals, man has a body (khet) animated by the universal spirit (BA). This becomes in him the animated soul, which is carried by his blood, and the loss of this soul causes his body to die."

"Like animals, he has a phantom-shadow, khaibit. Like them, he has several KA-qualities and vital forces, both organic and functional-nourished by the kau of food. Like higher animals, he has a lower KA, which includes the signatures and the innate and acquired characteristics of personality and all passionate, psychic, and organic animal impulses."

"Superior to animals, man has a higher KA which is his spiritual entity. This entity descends from the Maat (who is cosmic consciousness) and in man's consciousness becomes his own Maat."

"The higher KA comes in contact with the animal man through subtle nuclei-hidden nerve centers-that act as relays. It is attracted to the unborn child through affinity with the characteristics of the lower KA embodied in the embryo. (See commentary, #10.) After contact is made, it will become incarnate only if consciousness develops sufficient independence to give mastery over the lower KA to the individual. Ancient Egypt insistently offers men this aim: to achieve "conscious union of both KA so as to awaken the higher human reason and allow intuitive knowledge to be connected with ideas." (See Her-Bak, Vol II, Chap. XVIII)".

The comment above "Superior to animals, man...)" can be debated. Yes, man has the ability to reason and build things using science and mathematics. However, the way I see it, each animal, reptile, fish, insect has its own reality and universe which is closed to man's understanding. For example, a bee has its own reality and secrets which man cannot possibly fathom because he is not a bee. Man can study bees, learn a lot about their behavior, but will always remain closed to the bee's world and reality. There might be things about a bee man will never find out. Man loves to place himself above all other creatures, yet every creature has a reality which makes it unique. Thus, equality is more like it than separation because we all have that spark of life making each unique and adapted to its world.

"The divine element of man then can become fixed. The divine BA, his Horian soul, when attracted by the fulfilled total KA, forms a union that is the ultimate promise of immortality." (13).

"the animated soul, which is carried by his blood...";

The higher KA comes in contact with the animal man through subtle nuclei-hidden nerve centers-that act as relays..."

"It is attracted to the unborn child through affinity with the characteristics of the lower KA embodied in the embryo..."

Earlier, in commentary #10 De Lubicz states: "Maternal heredity plays the role of <u>substantive milieu</u> in the psychic makeup of the embryo, whereas paternal heredity plays the role of active essence giving the specific form of its lineage. So the child bears the signature of the reaction of his own KA to the two-fold hereditary influence. The heredity, however, has been chosen by the KA to present affinities corresponding to what it needs for living experiences, either to facilitate the expression of its essential tendencies or on the contrary to provide opportunities for struggles that may lead to acquisitions of consciousness." (14).

The above quotes seem to suggest a body-soul connection at a cellular level, the body itself being a platform for learning and testing in the physical world. Further driving home this cellular connection can be found in the following quote: "-snakes encircling mummies, showing the vital force for which the body was the support;" (15).

Now let's pause for a moment and think, really think about this last quote. What entwined "serpent" can be found in every cell of the human body?

DNA…Deoxyribonucleic acid, the very stuff of life on this planet. I do not believe that is was by chance that the Ancient Egyptians depicted snakes encircling mummies. Initiates knew what that represented, and knew that the KA interacted at a cellular level right down to the DNA.

How did they know? How do shamans throughout the world know the symbolic meaning of the serpent?

There seems to be a universal knowledge of serpents. This knowledge may very well go back to the beginning of life on this planet as Harner experienced through his vision of the dragon. DNA may be the divine transmitter, the seat of our soul, which the Ancient Egyptians knew existed; and this may explain why the Ancient Egyptians preserved their dead.

The Divine Coil

NIH is involved today with an ongoing project called the Genome Project. Briefly, this project's goal is to map the entire human DNA molecule. The goal is to identify genes and lock on to specific genes which cause various diseases. Peripheral interests include finding the gene responsible for aging as an example. The project's goal in completing the mapping ranges from the year 2002 to 2010.

The Genome Project is being monitored by medical ethicists throughout the United States. Furthermore, independent watchdogs are also closely monitoring the projects as well.

The Genome Project then seems quite straight forward: identify the "bad boy" genes, find cures for diseases and have mankind live happily forever after. This is what is being sold to the public.

To me, the Genome Project seems like a modern Archon venture with a completely different agenda. Though I cannot prove it, some cracks have shed light through the veneer of science.

For example:

-Many countries can work secretly without bothering with monitoring agencies. Mainland China is an example of such a country.

-Human cloning attempts and child sex determination research has broke through into the media in heated debates.

-Periodic, persistent articles and books pop up on the issue of the "aging gene" or the "death gene". Honey-like hypotheses are ventured with the promise that human beings might live longer and healthier in the future. The promises stop short of immortality; however, one feels a very strong undercurrent in this interest.

Let's look at immortality for a moment. This raises many ethical issues such as: who would decide who lives forever: people in power? The very rich? Gifted people? If a select group of people were allowed immortality, wouldn't there be a backlash? Underground "immortality labs" would appear triggering legislation and laws banning such activities. An elite would be created. Eventually, the masses would rise triggering a revolution. Then immortality would be available to everyone, but at what cost? Populations would grow, food supplies would shrink, water would become scarce, promises of outer world colonization would be made. What if that didn't happen? Who would decide who dies?

This is just one example of the consequences of gene tampering. Science fiction, you say, but let's not forget how Captain Nemo's submarine became a reality in the modern world…some loaded with thermonuclear tipped missiles.

The focus of all this heated debate is the remarkable and mysterious DNA molecule. Imagine a twisted ladder forming a double helix, the ladder sidepieces made of sugar-phosphate, the inside ladder rungs made up of four nitrogen bases adenine, cytosine, guanine and thymine. (16). Adenine and Guanine are purines, cytosine and thymine belong to the pyrimidine class. This is important to know because:

1. The space between the two helically coiled phosphate=sugar chains allows effective hydrogen bonding only between a purine and a pyrimidine base. Two pyrimidines would be too far apart, and two purines would be squeezed too close together.
2. The strongest hydrogen bonding occurs between the A-T and G-C purine-pyrimidine pairs. The A-C and G-T pairs are less strongly attracted to one another." (17).

One should not confuse DNA and RNA. RNA is a single-stranded, divided into messenger RNA, transfer RNA and ribosomal RNA all involved in protein synthesis. Adenine, cytosine, guanine and uracil make up the four bases of RNA.

RNA viruses are viruses that use RNA as their genetic material. Examples are SARS, influenza, hepatitis C, Hepatitis E, West Nile fever, polio, measles and Covid 19.

Remarkably, DNA can replicate itself by "unzipping" the double helix, each strand becoming a template for what is called a daughter strand. It's precise replication is a computer like, elegant in its simplicity.

Just like the Hopi altar, scientist can disassemble the DNA molecule in its component parts. Missing, however, is the ignition key. Of course, genes can be identified, catalogued. But something still eludes comprehension.

What eludes us might be found in the cutting edge of research involving energy and biological systems. This research is extremely exciting and promises breakthroughs in the understanding of life and its spiritual link to a Higher Power.

All life is awash in energy, mostly in light form. Mae-Wan Ho and Fritz-Albert Popp, in their paper titled Biological Organization, Coherence, and Light Emission from Living Organisms (18), state that "Light is generally emitted from an excited atom or molecule, when an electron in the outermost orbital, having absorbed a quantum of energy, is prompted to a higher energy level. The excited atom or molecule can then undergo a chemical reaction, or the electron can relax back to the ground state radiatively, by emitting a photon, or nonradiatively, by a transfer of phonons (sound waves) or by giving off the energy as heat." (19). Energy is found at different levels: "The lowest energy band involved in bonding-the valency band- is filled with electrons. The next higher band is the conduction band to which electrons can be promoted by absorbing energy such as heat or light. Electrons in this band are the mobile charge carriers. Between the highest valency level and the lowest conduction level lies the <u>band gap</u>, corresponding to the threshold of energy which must be absorbed to promote a valency electron to a conducting one. Thus, excitation always involves a separation of charges. If the excited electron is not conducted away, it may relax back to the ground state (to recombine with the positively charged "hole" left behind) by radiating a photon or nonradiatively as described above. Another source of photons in a solid state system is from "excitons", i.e., an excited electron-hole pair which can propagate over long distances before giving up energy by emitting a photon." (20). This long quote was necessary in order to build the groundwork for the following: Rattemeyer and Popp (48, Rattemeyer, M., and F.A. Popp. "Evidence of Photon Emission from DNA in Living Systems". Naturwissenschaften 68 (1981): S572-S573.) suggested that the DNA molecule is an excited duplex, or exciplex, in which photons are stored and, hence, can be a source of biophotons. Exciplex formation in DNA has been shown to predominate even at room temperature. (64, Vigny, P., nd M. Duquesne. "On the Fluorescence Properties of Nucleotides and Polynucleotides at Room Temperature." In "Excited States of Biological Molecules", edited by J.B. Birks, 167-177. London: Wiley, 1976.) So it is not surprising that living systems could emit light from processes taking place all over the cell. (21). Though self emission is too weak to analyze, "In connection with the trapping on storage of photons, it has been observed that death in organisms is invariably initiated by an intense light emission (at least three orders of magnitude above the self-emission rate) which can go on for more than 48 hours. (35, Li, K.H., F.A. Popp, W. Nagl, and H. Klima. "Indications of Optical Coherence in Biological Systems and its Possible Significance." In Coherent Excitations in Biological Systems, edited by H. Frohlich and F. Kremer, 117-122. Berlin: Springer-Verlag, 1983. And 41, Neurohi, R. Unpuplished observation, 1989.)" (22).

The implications of this research are enormous. Energy emission from cells, as stated above, is too weak to measure; conventional science has dismissed, so far, any such notion because the energy is almost immeasurable. Yet, what about energy? How much do we really know?

What makes a school of fish move in unison instantly? Can cells communicate the same way?

Can they communicate <u>universally</u>?

If we reflect, for a moment, what was discussed earlier relating to parallel universes, this notion of instant, universal communication could be a reality. How, we don't know. The notion that we live in a serpentine universe, containing, within our cells, the very essence of this serpentine creative energy, spells, perhaps, the concept that <u>communication</u> could be <u>instantaneous</u> <u>universally</u>. By observing life on earth, one can discover the very secrets of the universe; for example the school of fish moving <u>instantly</u> in unison. If one goes beyond what that scene represents, one can understand that communication at a cellular level can occur. And going beyond, cellular interdimensional communication could occur also, <u>instantly</u>.

<u>Ancient Records</u>

In 1985, Svante Paablo extracted over 3,000 mitochondrial DNA subunits from a 2,400 year old Egyptian mummy of a child using the Polymerase Chain Reaction which enables scientists today to clone off DNA. (23). Chromosomal DNA, from the nucleus of the cell, would be better, because it would represent the genetic code of both parents versus the mitochondrial DNA which is maternal. The far reaching implications, as techniques get better, is that archeologists could trace the origins of the Ancient Egyptians. By building a "genetic tree", one could go far back in time.

The problem still facing scientists lies in the reconstruction of a complete DNA molecule. A little over six billion units of four different types of units make up the human genetic code. (24). Reconstructing a dinosaur like in the movie Jurassic Park is still a very big stretch because of damage DNA suffers over time. Cloning Ramses the Great is not something which could be achieved in the near future. There is still, however, the possibility, given new breakthroughs in genetic research, that such a dream might become a reality someday.

Here lies the potential of immortality which opens a host of unanswerable questions. For one, given a perfect copy, would the KA of Ramses the Great re-enter his clone? Would his BA follow? What would happen if Ramses the Great was cloned at the time his incarnation was living...would that incarnation die in order to release the soul of Ramses the Great? Or would <u>another</u> soul copy be made from the genetic clone...

One thing is certain: given the snake symbology the Ancient Egyptians held sacred, genetic knowledge was somehow known to them, and this knowledge was directly connected to the soul.

The fragments of old DNA perhaps hold an essence of that living person today. Just like an ancient record, it lies dormant until technology comes along to release its secrets.

Unfortunately, science has not yet linked spirituality with its quest for knowledge. Spirituality is still very much distanced from science. This is highly disturbing, because what science probes is spiritual; everything science examines comes from creational power. As long as science ignores this fact, certain truths will be blocked from the seekers. Geneticists will successfully break down and analyze the DNA molecule but if they fail to "see" the DNA beyond its genetic record, they might miss DNA's creational origin.

The sudden burst of energy at the moment of death of an organism might explain how DNA stores energy in the form of photons which are important in maintaining life. Residual energy within the DNA molecule might be what the Ancient Egyptians referred to as the KA. The sun is the source of photons, hence, the source of the life force within DNA. The sun played an important role in Ancient Egyptian cosmology; it was the source of life for both the living and the dead. The connection between the sun's energy being channeled to the serpent through the goddess (and the Hopi women channeling the setting sun's energy into the plaques) makes sense in the light of the sun's role in keeping the DNA energized through life. Upon death, the sun enters the picture as a sanctuary to those who can read the road map and clues left by the living. Possibly, the residual energy/KA acts as a battery base for the BA in order to facilitate its journey in the hereafter. Considering the body's breakdown post death, it can only be temporary unless the body is preserved, thus preserving the DNA as well. With preservation, time is gained relating to the BA's journey.

So far, I have discussed the possibility that the DNA molecule is the seat of the KA, and perhaps also the BA. Where does this leave the Creator? Given the possibility of universal communication and the maxim "as above, so below", this universe itself might be one mind with a "central command". Are all other universes under the same command? Possibly, and possibly not. These imponderables will probably remain so for a very, very long time. We as a specie, might never know. One thing is clear: the very secrets of the universe are right here on earth provided one knows where to look.

It seems to me that all DNA, both living and dead, constitute and ancient record. We have, within our DNA, the record of our ancestors. "the animated soul, which is carried by his blood..." (25) gives a hint to the ancient record. The record extends deep in time before human beings walked the earth. Perhaps its origin lie with the dragon beings with which Harner communicated through his vision.

There seems to be a common theme relating to the soul throughout cultures: immortality. There is also a promise of an afterlife as well within a spiritual world of great beauty and perfection. This, I believe, is the original gift of the Creator not only to man but to all life. Life is a continuum that goes on in infinity and mirrors its Creator. Whatever happens to the soul after physical death is a great mystery. I believe, however, that it is a beautiful mystery full of love and compassion and not man's concoction of punishment and retribution. Today, someone asked me if I believe in Jesus, the Son of God. What struck me is that God, within the Judeo-Christian system is always referred to as a He/Son/Father. Never is God referred to in the feminine. Perhaps this stems from the concept of the original sin in the Garden of Eden. I have to agree with the Gnostics that this concept of the original sin is flawed and false. I see the Creator incorporating both the male and female aspects. So no, I don't believe in the Son of God, but rather in a one Creator Who encompasses the male and female energies and Who creates out of love and compassion.

The serpent/dragon might be the closest representation of the Creator of this universe and perhaps of all universes. The serpent represents primeval power; we have a vestige of this power within our reptilian primitive brain stem. It is from there that the dragons communicated their message to Harner. The Hopi Snake/Antelope dance is one of many snake rituals found throughout the world. There is a reason. And the reason might be to remind us of our origin at the beginning of time.

Jeremy Narby, in his book The Cosmic Serpent, DNA and the Origins of Knowledge explores how Shamans in South America use extremely powerful tobacco which in turn stimulates neuro receptors through which they communicate with an internal Serpent regarding what to do to heal a patient. Narby further explores the DNA molecule and its potential as a cosmic radio which Shamans tap into under the influence of nicotine.

Perhaps this origin, buried within our DNA is something feared by modern Archons. Locked away a long time ago, this origin might be revealed through modern technology. We can only hope that the truth of our spiritual origin will be revealed; and this revelation will make us free.

CHAPTER SEVEN

THE PLACE OF REEDS

"Indra's Net".

"There is an endless net of threads throughout the Universe.

The horizontal threads are in space; the vertical threads in time.

At every crossing of threads there is an individual, and every individual is a crystal bead.

The great light of Absolute Being illuminates and penetrates every crystal bead.

And also, every bead reflects not only the light from every other crystal in the net.

But also every reflection of every reflection throughout the Universe."

From The Message of the Crystal Skull quoting a Veda of Ancient India. (1).

Instantaneous, universal and outer-dimensional communication may be possible through what North American Indians refer to as Grandmother Spider's Web which consists of an energy grid encircling the earth. (2). This web, or net, shows itself on a mural at Edfu, the place of reeds.

The original, primitive reed temple which was described earlier had its origin with a mound, the Primeval Mound, which surfaced from the Primeval Waters. Order at that point began. A split reed became the perch for the Divine Falcon around which a reed temple was built. This perch, part of what is known as the Djed Pillar was the focal point, the sacred palladium of the primitive temple.

Barbara Watterson, in her book The House of Horus at Edfu states that the earliest shrines in Ancient Egypt were built out of reed and mud.

None have survived. Yet, this original plan persisted when temples were built with stone:

"Stone columns were copies of the supports made from tree trunks or bundles of plant-stems that were used in the earliest buildings. Accordingly, stone columns often have five bands carved bellow the capital, imitating the thongs which with which the bunches of stems in the original forms were held together. Many of the plants used to make early forms of column must sometimes have flowered despite no longer being planted in the ground; and it is probably this flowering that inspired some of the decoration of the capitals of stone columns. The varieties of capital employed reflect their vegetable origin, being carved to represent palm-fronds, lotus buds and papyrus umbels; and in the Ptolemic and Roman periods, especially, the campaniform capital, a composite derived from many varieties of flower, real and imaginary, was popular." (3).

At Edfu, reeds themselves throughout, engraved in stone. It seems that reeds, (after an unforgettable event which manifested through legends throughout the world as the flood), became a powerful symbol of post flood resurrection. Reeds enabled survivors to construct boats in order to fish. Reed boats of similar construction can be found from Lake Titicaca to the Nile. Reeds play a prominent role in the emergence myths of the Hopi. And reeds are found throughout the architecture of the temple at Edfu.

It seems that reeds symbolized life. The djed pillar, on which the perch of reed was constructed for the falcon was a sacred link to the lost world of the Seven Builder Gods as E.A.E. Reymond outlined in her brilliant book The Mythical Origin of the Egyptian Temple. So if the djed pillar was a link to the lost world, then, can we safely presume that the reed was also an important symbol of the lost world's inhabitants. Why? Was there a legend of a <u>previous</u> destruction of another world? Was the reed, in that lost world, a reminder of a <u>previous</u> destruction at an extremely remote time in history? Was the reed a symbol of its resurrection as well?

Strangely, Indra's net quoted at the beginning of this chapter closely parallels what was discussed in Chapter five. "The horizontal threads are in space; the vertical threads in time." (4). strangely hints to a higher form of physics of "space and time." The Net at Edfu hints at space and time again; and the North American Indians refer to an energy grid encircling the earth like a spider's web. The parallels are just too close to call them coincidence. Reed symbology falls into the same pattern. Above the Net at Edfu are engraved reeds, bulrushes. Reeds play a vital role during the emergence myth of the Hopis. The reed boats on lake Titicaca closely resembles reed boats on the Nile. Reeds, woven together, create a diamond pattern, a net, and reeds are profusely represented on the walls of the Temple of Edfu. It is possible that a message was intentionally left within the symbology of the common reed pointing to a high form of physics that only an elite group from a lost world could camouflage so skillfully and persist through the entire history of Ancient Egypt. And to make sure the message did not get lost, reed symbology was also sprinkled in North and South America.

The Ancient Egyptian Pyramid Texts might give us a glimpse to the meaning of what reeds represent. There are references to a ferryman (Utterance 475), sky doors (Utterance 563), an ascension to a portal (Utterance 594). In Utterance 519, the ferryman is referred to as a "gate-keeper of Osiris" (5).

Numerous references of barks and reed-floats are scattered throughout the text. But as I read the Ancient Pyramid Texts (which can be very tedious indeed!) I got a peripheral feel of the hidden meaning behind the words. Some texts brought this out more than others, like Utterances 519 and 520. It seems that I was reading a star map for an interdimensional voyage.

I find the Ancient Pyramid Texts extremely strange. They seem to cast a spell. The reading eventually becomes intuitive. This intuition becomes a key which unlocks doorways.

In Utterance 473 titled The King crosses the celestial river (6), reed-floats appear to come down from the Day-bark and the Night-bark. Are these barks some kind of mother ship from which reed-floats descend from? A long, cylindrical object in the sky would appear like a reed; are we reading the description of a star ship?

The hieroglyphics of the text themselves could very well have been written in code. Barbara Watterson states in her book The House of Horus at Edfu that Ptolemaic hieroglyphic script was written in code, the meaning of which, to this day, has yet to be deciphered. (7). Possibly the coding technique was known when the Ancient Egyptian Pyramid texts were written. Another view which was proposed by Graham Hancock in his book The Fingerprints of the Gods suggests that at the time the Ancient Egyptian Pyramid Texts were written, the original texts from which they were copied were, in themselves, extremely ancient and written in another language altogether. (8). Possibly these ancient texts differed from the Ancient Egyptian Pyramid texts in that an attempt was made to translate the original texts which might explain the numerous, obscure nature of some of the passages in the present version. Possibly a little translation difficulties and coding occurred when the texts were inscribed on the walls of the pyramid of Unas. What we have today through Falkner's brilliant work are texts still partially coded through which glimpses of meaning break through.

The Shemsu-Hor were described as having fingers of iron, or were made of iron. (9). Armor? If armor, then what were the Shemsu-Hor protecting themselves from? Did they ride the "reed-floats" from mother ships?

Earlier, I had mentioned Spider Woman packing Hopi ancestors in reeds with water and white cornmeal for sustenance. Were the reeds a type of stellar ark? Did they appear like reeds in the sky? It was also mentioned that the Hopi Ancestors looked for a land with aid of a giant reed; a telescope? And when the Hopi Ancestors emerged into the Fourth World through a reed, was that emergence their exiting from a reed like from a spacecraft?

And what of the sky doors, the portals mentioned in the Ancient Egyptian Pyramid Texts; do they represent interdimensional gates through which the ferryman/gate-keeper navigated?

There is no doubt as evidenced by Graham Hancock, Robert Bauval and Adrian Gilbert's work that the Ancient Egyptian Pyramid Texts point to a stellar cult. The mathematical evidence presented in The Message of the Sphinx and in The Orion Mystery show the relationships between the Giza Plateau and the stars. Furthermore, Graham Hancock presents further evidence in Fingerprints of the Gods relating to the Ancient Egyptian Pyramid Texts and the stars. I say evidence, because to this date I have not seen any strong rebuttal from the academic world. Actually, the academic world is silent vis a vis the evidence presented by these authors. Why? Because the case which was built around the evidence is just too strong; the evidence is backed by astronomical data. Yet, Egyptologists currently and steadfastly refuse to acknowledge any of the evidence presented by these authors.

I use the word evidence freely because that's exactly what Graham Hancock, Robert Bauval and Adrian Gilbert have presented. The word evidence probably grates the nerves of current Egyptologists. However, that's too bad. Egyptologists should carefully review the data. Yet, I believe they never will, because the evidence will eventually crumble their carefully built hypotheses and theories. Too many reputations are at stake, too much hubris is present as well. To acknowledge the work of outsiders would be too much to ask.

My presentation, on the other hand, is speculative. Yet, speculation is healthy; it makes one think. It gives a different spin on the meaning of what was written a long, long time ago. When one begins to crack a code, one starts by brainstorming. Someone else reading my ideas might have a sudden insight; that person might break the code. Perhaps someone might expand on my ideas which might eventually lead to a breakthrough. That's why the written word is so important, no matter how small, or insignificant it might be.

However speculative my ideas are relating to the reed/starship link, I feel that I'm not too far from the truth. The survivor gods may have come from a lost world on earth, an outpost to a lost world in space. And perhaps that lost world might have been an outpost in itself. Mars, as discussed by Graham Hancock in his book The Mars Mystery may have been that space outpost which was devastated by a cosmic cataclysm.

It is difficult for people to accept such a hypothesis because of our conditioned, ethno-centric view of ourselves. This conditioning is steeped in social and religious views. These views are very hard to change. They are so hard, in fact, that if evidence of an interstellar contact was revealed today, the facts themselves would be attacked, and in some circles actually dismissed. Religious fervor would demonize the findings in an attempt to distance humanity from the facts. These attempts to control our thoughts through carefully scripted history and religious dogma still occurs today, even in societies which pride themselves to be free in thought and word.

Edfu, the place of reeds, was not designed haphazardly. The temple was carefully built to reconstruct, down to the slightly elevated floor of the inner sanctuary, the primeval temple in the place of reeds. But with everything

Ancient Egyptians have presented so far, reeds not only signify the first place of reeds and building material of the first temple but also signify a stellar connection as well. I also get the sense that primary documents were available to the priesthood, from the original texts the Ancient Egyptian Pyramid Texts were copied from to later ones discovered in archives. New knowledge was added to the spiritual base over the years. Perhaps the rites of mummification stems from an original source, a very ancient source of stellar origin.

The strange practice of Canopic equipment which consisted of jars in which embalmed organs were preserved goes back to the time of Kheops. (10). Prior to this period, the preservation of dead bodies can be traced to the Archaic Period, (11). Earlier, I suggested that the Ancient Egyptians may have wanted to preserve something within the mortal remains (DNA?) in order for the KA to magnetically hang, so to speak, in close proximity to the mortal remains.

I've always viewed embalmed bodies and Canoptic equipment as something akin to deep hibernation for a very long stellar journey. The pyramid may have played a part, the meaning of which, to this date, is lost.

Yet, let's explore this a little further. Many believe that pyramids accumulated power, energy, which I suspect comes from the sun in the form of photons. A box which was designed to house canopic jars was "found in the floor of the sepulchral chamber of the Second Pyramid of Giza" (12). This box "is cut hard against the south wall of the chamber, south-east of the sarcophagus. (13). Unfortunately, many other such caches have been obliterated by looters, so it is difficult to determine any consistency to this practice in many pyramids. Graham Hancock himself stated that the Great Pyramid was never intended to be a tomb; that the architecture lends more towards a temple, a stellar marker of unknown purpose and practice.

Perhaps pyramids were both a temple and a place where mortal embalmed remains were brought in. This might have been, because if the pyramid acts as a gigantic accumulator of photon energy, then it could have been used to "irradiate" the embalmed remains with photon energy.

Recently, I saw a news brief on research being done using DNA as a means to conduct electric current. Furthermore, the researchers were commenting on how the DNA strand acts as an accumulator. It is possible that DNA might be used some day as a molecular capacitator.

This research is very exciting in supporting my thesis that Ancient Egyptians knew this from a very old source. By "irradiating" DNA with photon energy, within an accumulator which the pyramid lends itself as, then this excited DNA within the embalmed mortal remains insured the KA's magnetic link to the body and the BA. Though this stellar journey is still not very clear, it points to a stellar origin of incredible power.

We, as human beings, are hollow reeds in a sense, metaphysically speaking. We strive to connect with a divine source throughout our lives in order to make sense of our ultimate fate: death. The Ancient Egyptians attempted to communicate through redundant symbols which were loaded with metaphysical, and perhaps, technological meaning. At the Temple of Edfu, reeds are repeated over and over again throughout the architecture. The reed was the transport mechanism for the elect Hopi ancestors guided by Spider Woman to a new land after a cataclysmic event. Both cultures were "reed driven" after a cataclysmic event which brought both cultures to the first land. The first Pre Dynastic temple of Ancient Egypt was built out of reeds. The tsotsokpi, the perch, for the souls of departed Hopi society members, "the dead have power over rain" (Armin W. Geertz, Hopi Indian Altar, P 27), and the Djed pillar on which the falcon perches on, the medicine bowl in the sand ridge...the first mound of the first time in the Egyptian Temple. Two cultures with similar myths and rituals: such repetition can only signify one thing-pay close attention.

The place of reeds then, at Edfu, has many layered meanings. From a reconstruction in stone of the primitive, reed temple, to the Net which I linked to interdimensional physics all create a very layered tapestry of meaning interwoven with legends including the cosmic origin of Edfu written in a book which came from the sky, as well as the Ancestral Hopi elect, brought to their new land in a reed...The place of reeds extends in the Ancient Egyptian Pyramid Texts. This constant repetition can only mean that reeds themselves mean more than building material and the primeval marsh of the First Time. The continuous Hopi rituals within various Hopi societies in their kivas, year after year for centuries, all, can only represent one thing: a physics of high order of Space and Time.

CHAPTER EIGHT

THE HERE AND NOW

March, 2020

Shemsu-Hor was researched and written during the early 1990's.

Many things have transpired since, and today, March 19, 2020, in East Lansing Michigan, my wife Laurel and I, to include my daughter Sara and children in Boston, MA and Alison and children in Franklin, TN, and Laurel's relatives in Philadelphia, Chicago, and Canada are all witnessing the effects of a 0.1 micron virus named Covid 19 causing sickness and death including its dismantling of the world's economy in a systematic, brutal fashion.

A virus, 0.1 micron in size.

Laurie Garrett, in her book The Coming Plague, Newly Emerging Diseases in a World Out of Balance (Copyright 1994) warned that emerging diseases would appear as well as old ones believed to be suppressed. Articles found on the Internet also speak of the release of ancient bacteria and viruses, locked in ice for thousands of years, released by the melting of those glaciers into the world with potential pandemic results. Scientists do caution that most of these ancient bacteria and viruses are harmless. But it only takes one bad boy awakening from its deep slumber to cause a massive pandemic worldwide.

The cause of this world wide melt down is, I believe, caused by a cosmic event affecting the earth right now.

"On December 30th, 1983, NASA's chief Scientist of the Infra-Red Astronomical Satellite telescope (IRAS) announced that NASA had discovered Planet X.

Just one week after the story of Planet X was released, the magazine US News and World Report ran a story retracting the announcement and NASA has been silent ever since.

That did not stop Dr Robert S. Harrington who was the chief astronomer of the US Naval Observatory until his mysterious death in 1993.

By analyzing an extensive amount of publications relating to Planet X, in chronological order, not only does the cover up of Planet X become extraordinary, but one gains a unique perspective of the evaluation of the Planet X discovery.

The following is a comprehensive collection of excerpts from Planet X articles dating back to the 1950's. Pay close attention to the tone of each article as the theories progress. (The Planet X Cover-up in the Mainstream Media Yowusa.com, 18 March 2012, Justin Braithwaite).

The article is still on line as of March 19 2020.

Another strange occurrence going on is a shifting of the North Magnetic Pole. An NPR article February 2, 2019, titled "The North Magnetic Pole is shifting East, Fast" with NPRs Ari Shapiro speaking with Nature reporter Alex Witze: "There's some strange movement at the top of the globe right now. The north magnetic pole, which has been used for navigation for centuries, is shifting east-and it's shifting fast."

For those who wonder what affects the magnetic pole, that answer lies with the molten core of the earth. What could be causing an effect on the molten core?

In www.whitewolfpack.com/2015/04/earth-has-shifted, "Earth has shifted" Inuit elders issue warning to NASA and the world (video).

This brings me to Richard Sauder's works, "Underground Bases and Tunnels, What is the Government trying to hide?", "Underwater & Underground Bases: Surprising Facts the Government Does Not Want You to Know", and "Hidden in Plain Sight: Beyond the X-Files".

I have followed this underground drilling project and what I discovered is that this project has been going on for over forty years…What did the Government know back then that is affecting planet earth today?

Graham Hancock, in his book "The Mars Mystery" "makes a strong case that NASA is motivated by a lingering Cold War mentality and fear that evidence of alien life will have a destabilizing political, economic, and social consequences. In exploring the traces left by the Martian civilization and the cosmic cataclysm that may have ended it, The Mars Mystery is both an illumination of our ancient past and a warning-which we still have time to heed-about our ultimate fate."

Are we, right now, approaching a cosmic rendez vous-again?

Leo Tanguma created the new Denver Airport Murals and some are quite terrifying-one shows a fireball streaking in the sky as terrified people huddle while a soldier dressed in a green uniform holding a sword pointed to a dove, holding a rifle his left hand towering over the huddled people while buildings in the distance are being cratered...

The New Denver Airport is believed to be a portal to Sauder's underground world...

What does the Government know and what is it hiding?

In the book "When Stars came Down to Earth Cosmology of the Skidi Pawnee Indians of North America" by Von Del Chamberlain, on page 143 Figure 36, "Evidence suggests that the traditional Plains feather bonnet symbolized a comet."

On page 144, "In "How the World is to Come to an End," Dorsey (1906a:134-137) recorded the following belief: "Among the stars would be many signs. Meteors would fly through the sky." The story also indicated an awareness of meteor showers that had occurred in the past:

"My grandchild, some of the signs have come to pass. The stars have fallen among the people but the Moving Star is good to us, for we continue to live....Our people were made by the stars. When the time comes for all things to end our people will turn into small stars and will fly to the South Star, where they belong. When the time comes for the ending of the world the stars will again fall to the earth. They will mix among the people, for it will be a message to the people to get ready to be turned into stars."

It's happened before and it will happen again.

I would like to share some "Fireball Logs" from the American Meteor Society starting with Fireball Sightings worldwide beginning in 2008:

2008   52
2009   43
2010   64

2011	146
2012	201
2013	386
2014	399
2015	580
2016	589
2017	5490
2018	5965
2019	6926
2020	1328 so far as of March 2020

Are we approaching a zone in space where a debris field is following a celestial body (Planet X?)? It may be the same visitor to our solar system identified by the IRAS system in 1983, which, in the remote past wiped out Mars pushing it into a new orbit, and causing cataclysmic events on earth that many surviving civilizations have not forgotten and recorded in their legends, myths, religious texts and engravings on rock.

Von Del Chamberlain states on page 208-"A few things should be said in conclusion to emphasize the more important results of this study. It seems apparent that the Skidi Pawnee had a complex religious system that was based upon interpretations of observed natural phenomena. The objects and phenomena of the sky and the repetitive relationships between them had a special significance; indeed, the uniqueness of Skidi intellectual life seems to have been based upon their fascination with and knowledge about the sky. Their interest in the sky was fundamental; whereas most other Indian groups supposed their origins to have been from the earth, the Skidi looked overhead to find their ancestors."

The Skidi Pawnee considered meteorites sacred and kept them in sacred bundles. They were very keen at studying the sky intently and had Skidi Pawnee star chart. Were they also possibly tracking fireball and observing stellar positions based on their frequency?

In his chapter 26 Dark Star, "The Mars Mystery", Graham Hancock quotes Sir Fred Hoyle on page 272 regarding the myopic stance of NASA regarding meteorites and comets:

"It could be seen as curious that society would seek to investigate distant galaxies while at the same time ignoring all possibility of serious impacts with Earth, surely a clear example of amnesia in action," (Hoyle, Origin of Universe, 62.)

I'm suspicious in nature; is it possible that the Covid 19 event is a massive distraction, focusing people's attention <u>away</u> from the sky, getting people instead scope locked on a 0.1 micron virus…It's just a hypothesis, but observing what is happening on earth and the <u>increased</u> number of fireballs sighted since 2008 seems to me that we are approaching something way bigger than Covid 19, something which makes the underground cities built for over 40 years pointing to a threat from above, from the sky, as Indicated by Skidi Pawnee warnings of a future event regarding falling stars from the sky.

To be clear, Covid 19 was identified as a virus which jumped species. Indications point to a Chinese market yet research point to bats being carriers. The origin of Covid 19 is yet to be determined definitely, and the beginning point of the outbreak has receded in the past quickly as the outbreak spread throughout the world. The virus has caused severe economic hardship, and some countries have dealt with the outbreak in an outstanding way, others, like the United States have shown an abysmal response to the point of ignoring it and labeling it "just another virus". The United States have states within, some of which, like Michigan, under the governance of Gretchen Whitmer have done an excellent job in containing the outbreak. Other states like Florida have acted in a way that is to me criminal regarding preparedness and response.

Covid 19 has captured the attention of everyone causing a hibernation state while everyone is waiting for a vaccine. The vaccine is the only way out of this puzzle, this captivity. Yet, as everyone focuses on Covid 19, earth changes have been put on the back burner such as the California fires caused by weather pattern and global changes.

As of today, September 30 2020, fireball events total 5410, per the fireball logs of the American Meteor Society. It was 1328 in March, 2020.

Thus, as we focus within, we are not focusing outward.

The ancient builders did not build building with mathematical precision because they had nothing else to do. As I mentioned, stone weathers very slowly, and the structures maintain their mathematical message pretty much intact over thousands of years. There was a warning coded in those structures. What has happened will happen again.

Government continuation and the elite will be safe in the underground cities in the United States and in other countries. In Richard Sauder's book, "Underground Bases and Tunnels, What is the government trying to hide?" (copyright 1995), he states the following in his afterword:

"Any reader of this book ought to come away with at least this one, basic understanding: the Pentagon is definitely heavily involved in and interested in underground facilities. There is no doubt about that.

A number of other non-military agencies are involved as well. The Department of Energy (DOE), the Federal Emergency Management Agency (FEMA), the National Security Agency (NSA), the Colorado School of Mines, and the Federal Reserve are some of the known underground players.

And there are Fortune 500 companies that have underground facilities. AT&T has a number of sophisticated underground centers. Northrop, Lockheed and McDonnel Douglas have hi-tech underground centers in California. Standard Oil at one time had a command post deep underground in New York State. There may be others operated by other companies."

Sauder's books outline an incredibly organized and coordinated underground operation hidden in the open which has been going on for decades. Some access points, like the new Denver Airport are hidden in the open as well. You may have passed one without knowing it. Yet, try to access that underground world-you will need a "passport" and if you have a need to know today you are part of the project. But the majority of "passport" holders do not know as of yet that they are invited guests to this underground world until they get the call.

What I gather from many sources and leaked information from workers these underground cities are massive. They have condos, parks, cafes, malls, fountains, restaurants, stores. I would not be surprised to find Starbucks cafes in those underground cities. The power supplied is probably nuclear near a huge water source, underground.

I also understand that an underground shipping zone where semi trucks go to around the clock in Missouri is a supply access to this underground world.

So these underground facilities beg again an explanation regarding their massive expense over decades in drilling out, engineering and construction. Why would the United States and other countries do this? What was the triggering information which started such massive building?

Planet X was leaked in 1983 but perhaps the information was known even before that date. What I gather, sifting through a lot of information regarding Planet X is that the main culprit of its periodic passing is a massive bombardment of meteorites on earth from its tail, its debris field following its passage. The one mural at the new Denver airport painted by Leo Tanguma, showing a massive meteor in the sky with a soldier holding a sword is a telling clue.

The picture is frightening regarding the celestial body, the huddled people, the soldier indicating Martial law, the damaged buildings. The dove at the point of the sword would indicate total domination by a government power.

Are we revisiting a period in history which affected the entire world in the past which caused ancient people to record the event in stone, legends, and in the keeping of sacred meteorites in bundles as a reminder, a warning, a message transmitted through the ages.

ENDNOTES

Introduction

1   R.A. Schwaller De Lubicz, «Sacred Science», page 111.
2   Plato, «Timaeus and Critias», Penguin Classics, 1977, page 36.
3   Armin W. Geertz, «Hopi Indian Altar Iconography, Iconography of Religions, Institute of Religious Iconography State University Groningen, Section X: North America, Fascicle Five, 1987», page 1 of Forward
4   Ibid., page 16.

Chapter One

1   Robert H. O'Connell, "The Emergence of Horus", JEA, Volume 69, 1983, page 72.
2   Armin W. Geertz, "Hopi Indian Altar Iconography, Iconography of Religions, Institute of Religious Iconography State University Groningen, Section X: North America, Fascicle Five, 1987", page 17.
3   Ekkehart Malotki and Michael Lomatuway'ma, "Maasaw: Profile of a Hopi God", American Tribal Religions Volume Eleven, page 255.
4   Ibid, pages 256-258.
5   Ibid, page 258.
6   Ibid, pages 251-252.
7   Wallace H, Black Elk and William S. Lyon, PH.D, "Black Elk" page 192.
8   Ibid, pages 89-90.
9   R.O. Falkner, "The Ancient Egyptian Pyramid Texts", Utterance 466, page 155.

10 Von Del Chamberlain, "When Stars Came Down to Earth", page 146.

11 Ibid, page 144.

12 Ibid, page 143, part of caption of 2 photographs.

13 G.A. Wainwright, "The Origin of Storm-Gods in Egypt, JEW, Volume 49, 1963, page 14.

14 Ibid, page 14.

15 Graham Hancock, "The Mars Mystery", page 168.

16 Manetho, Translation by W.G. Waddell, "Manetho", page 191. (Publisher Harvard University Press, 1940).

17 Ibid, page 191.

18 G.A. Wainwright, "The Origin of Storm Gods in Egypt", JEA, Volume 49, 1963, page 15.

19 Robert Bauval and Adrian Gilbert, "The Orion Mystery:, page 211.

20 G.A. Wainwright, "The Origin of Storm Gods in Egypt", JEA, Volume 49, 1963, page 16.

21 Ibid, page 16.

22 E.A.E. Reymond, "The Mythical Origin of the Egyptian Temple".

Chapter Two

1 Armin W. Geertz, "Hopi Indian Altar Iconography", Iconography of Religions, Institute of Religious Iconography State University Groningen, Section X: North America, Fascicle Five, 1987, pages 22-23.

2 Ibid, page 24.

3 Ibid, page 24.

4 Ekkehart Malotki and Michael Lomatuway'ma, "Maasaw: Profile of a Hopi God", American Tribal Religions, Volume Eleven, pages 119-120.

5 Armin W. Geertz, "Hopi Indian Altar Iconography", Iconography of Religions, Institute of Religious Iconography State University Groningen, Section X: North America, Fascicle Five, 1987, page 20.

6 Ibid, page 19.

7 Ekkehart Malotki and Michael Lomatuway'ma, "Maasaw: Profile of a Hopi God", American Tribal Religions, Volume Eleven, page 43.

8 Armin W. Geertz, "Hopi Indian Altar Iconography", Iconography of Religions, Section X: North America, Fascicle Five, 1987, page 19.

9 Ibid, Page 19.

10 Ibid, page 20.

11 H.R. Voth, "The Oraibi Marau Ceremony" Field Museum of Natural History, Publication 156, Anthropological series, Vol. XI, No. 1, February 1912, pages 19-23.The Medicine Altar ritual presented here in the end notes is copied in its entirety only because I feel that including one part takes away the essence of the sacred. The ritual is one of many within the main ceremony.

"After a brief rest Wickwaya begins to put up the altar. He first places sand, previously gotten by Navini and a woman (see Plate IV, b), on the floor, forming it into a semi-circular ridge. Into this he inserts first the larger slabs and zigzags and then the smaller sticks and eagle feathers, and finally places all the smaller objects, the medicine bowl, ears of corn, et., into their proper places (see plate V). When the altar Is finished Wickwaya resumes his place in the corner with the two priestesses, the other participants also sitting in different parts of the kiva and waiting. At about two O'clock two of the priestesses, one of them Pungnyanomsi (No. 1), the other Ootchwuhti (No. 7), who acts as sprinkler, put on their white ceremonial robes, Wickwaya ties a nakwakwosi, of an eagle feather into their hair, and hands to each one the following objects: some nakwakwosis, some corn-meal, a long buzzard wing feather, a bone whistle, an ear of corn, one black baho, two green bahos, and a netted gourd vessel, and sends them to two different springs after water to be used in the ceremony. Following one of the priestesses to the spring Lanva (Flute Spring) I was enabled to note some details and to get some snapshot photographs. At the east side of the spring she stopped, held the prayer offerings to her lips and uttered a silent, short prayer. She then deposited the two bahos and three eagle feathers and one turkey feather nakwakwosi, with some sacred meal, I think in a small niche on the north side of the spring. Hereupon she descended to the spring proper. Which is about twenty feet below the level of the ground, and there, standing at the edge of the water (see Plate VII, a), blew the whistle several times towards the water. Then she imitated the act of dipping water with the whistle four times, with the long eagle feather five times and with the ear of corn four times, whereupon she filled the gourd vessel. She ascended the steps, taking with her the objects except the prayer offerings (see Plate VII, b). Arriving at the upper rim of the spring she cast a pinch of meal from the spring on the trail that leads to the village and deposited a "road" and some meal on the trail east of the spring, whereupon she hurried back to the kiva (see Plate VI, b), where she arrived in about fifteen minutes after she had left it. Here she waited on the east side of the ladder (see Plate VIII, a) until the other woman returned. The chief priest had in the meantime resumed his place in the corner. When they returned he met and greeted them, sprinkled first a meal line from the place where they were sitting to the altar, returned and took from them the small vessel with the water, the long feather and the whistle, and placed these objects on the floor at the altar, while the woman remained seated on the elevated portion of the kiva floor on the east side of the ladder, their feet resting on the floor of the deeper part of the kiva. The priest then stands in front of the women, holding some corn-meal in his right, a long buzzard wing feather in his left hand. He sprinkles some meal on the feathers, hums a song, beating time with the feather, waving it slightly up and down (see Plate VIII, b), circles it above their heads a few minutes and dusts off the meal towards the hatch-way. This he does six times. He then takes the nakwakwosis from their hair and places them with their mungwikuru, and resumes his place. His assistant hands him a so-called cloud blower, a cone-shaped pipe, which he fills with a certain kind of small, dry pine or spruce needles and places it on the floor near the altar. At about 3:15 P.M. all arrange themselves in a semicircle in front of the altar (see diagram on page 17).

The chief priest rises and goes through the same discharming performance as he did before with the two priestesses who fetched the water from the springs. The feather he circles this time in front of the altar over the heads of the participants in the ceremony. He then unties the nakwakwosis from the hair of the women, and places them on the floor in front of the altar, and then fills a smoke pipe with native tobacco which he also places on the floor, whereupon he squats down in front and about the middle of the altar, Navini and four women usually sitting on his left and four women on his right side. These ten persons are usually the ones that participates in the ceremonies around the altar, and hence are in this paper sometimes called leaders. Wickwaya then utters the following brief prayer:

"Taa, pai pi ita puu yep maksontota; owi yep itah mungwasi nanapangwani. Nap hakakwat unaywasyat nalo nananiwo tuikaowak put akv puma angk ichi palaye ak itamui okwatotwani.

Free Translation

"Now then, we exert ourselves (we are constrained); therefore we assist each other (cooperate) here in our concerns (offerings). From somewhere the four different ones (referring to the rain deities in the four world quarters) may they bring at the right time copious rains quickly (to us) taking pity on us."

Then the <u>first song</u> is begun (see Plate IX, a). Wickwaya beats time with a rattle, consisting of a short crook, to which a number of old cone shells are tied. His sister and her assistant beat time with gourd rattles and the rest with their ears of corn, which they call their "mothers". Navini, I think, beats time with a buzzard feather. During this song one of the women (No. 8) takes a tray with fine cornmeal and rubs four lines on the north, west, south and east wall of the kiva respectively, then throws a small pinch of meal against a joist over the altar and presses some to the floor east of the altar. Each of these acts is performed during one of the verses of the song.

The <u>second song</u> is then sung, during which the same woman takes a pinch of powder of some kind of a berry from the corn-husk, sprinkles it along the corn-ear and old makwanpi (aspergil) which are lying on the north side of the bowl into the bowl, picks up those two objects and holds both of them, point downward, into the medicine bowl and the pours some water on them from a netted gourd vessel. After having done this she asperges with them towards the altar and then replaces them. This she repeats with all the other ears of corn and aspergils.

The <u>third song</u> then follows. Another woman (No. 7) sprinkles a pinch of corn-pollen, I think, into the medicine bowl from the north side and then picks up an eagle bone whistle, bends over the medicine bowl and whistles into it (see Plate IX, b) asperging with the whistle when she is through. This she repeats from the other five directions.

During the <u>fourth song</u> another woman (No. 3) moves slightly forward in a kneeling position, picks up the ear of corn and makwanpi on the north side of the medicine bowl, dips then into a liquid and asperges. This she repeats with the remaining five corn-ears and makwanpis.

<u>Fifth song</u>. Two women (No. 2 and No. 10) each take the two old bow sticks, the one from the east, the other from the west side of the altar; another woman (No. 7) takes the two sticks with the grass wheels from the figurine on the west side, No. 9 takes those from the figurine on the east side of the altar, and all beat time with these objects on the floor. At a certain place of the song they raise them and with a sweeping, downward motion they dip them into the medicine bowl and then asperge with them towards the altar. When the dip their objects into the bowl all the others make a motion towards the bowl with the objects that they hold in their hands. All this is done six times.

<u>Sixth Song</u>. All sprinkle meal on the altar six times at short intervals. A short interruption now occurs in the singing, during which the chief priest takes a pinch of honey into his mouth, rises and takes the large cone-shaped pipe or cloud blower and lights it at the fireplace, whereupon the

<u>Seventh song</u> is commenced, during a part of which the chief priest blows smoke from the cloud blower over the altar and especially into the medicine bowl. The woman sitting at his right side (No. 7) shakes his shell rattle.

<u>A number of songs</u>, as nearly as I have been able to make out, eight, now follow, during which nothing is done except occasional asperging by the chief priest. Before the

<u>Ninth song</u> starts the chief priest steps behind the altar, the woman at the north-west corner of the altar (No. 1) (1) (1. In all the ceremonies, that I observed, this was Pungnyanomsi, the sister of Chief Lolulomaishe, as well as her older brother Shockhungyoma, is called Kik-mungwi (village chief) and they are said to "own the houses.") moving forward in a kneeling position.

To her the chief priest hands a stick which he takes from the sand ridge of the altar, swinging or moving it along the cotton string road on the altar and over the medicine bowl towards her, whereupon he resumes his seat. The singing is resumed, the woman beating time with one end of the stick on the floor. This stick, as well as the others in the sand ridge, is supposed to represent one of the dead members of the order (as is also the case with siilar sticks in other ceremonies), and it is believed that the striking of the floor announces to the deceased members in the nether world that a ceremony is in progress.

At a certain period of the song, when the word (wawayina (1) (1. Whether this is an old form for wangwaiyi, call, bekon; or whether wawayi-na, call (the) father, or waway-ina, call my father, is the correct etymology could not yet be fully determined,) occurs, she waves the stick in a horizontal circle from right to left and then continues to beat time on the floor. This she does seven times. (2) 2. This number seems to be unusual, six times, apparently, being the normal number. Why seven times I did not ascertain. But I have observed on other occasions that certain rites were performed seven times, where six would have seemed the regular number. Where the words are the same in each stanza it may sometimes ve an error.)

When the song is over all say thanks, the woman holds the stick with one end resting on the floor, and all wait in silence. The chief priest steps behind the altar, takes the stick from the woman, swings it backwards over the medicine bowl and along the string road towards himself, and replaces it and then resumes his seat. After a short silence he speaks a brief prayer: "Pay hapi ita yep maksontota; Owi itah maksoni akvmongwastotini." "Now (or well!) we exert (or trouble, constrain) ourselves here. And now our exertions shall be consummated," to which the others respond by saying, anxhaa (be it so). His assistant (Navini) lights a pipe and the two men smoke while the women take seats in different parts of the kiva.

The leaders fast on this day late in the evening; the other members abstain from salty foods only. The same rule applies also to the second, third and fourth day." The ceremony continues in a very complex manner. The important thing to note is the gathering of the water at the spring. Also note, for future reference, the netted gourd vessel.

(H.R. Voth did not understand several aspects, and recorded the <u>mechanical</u> aspects overall yet, as I mention, regarding the "ignition key" that initiated members would possess, only because they are born Hopi and members of that society, the secrets of the ceremony as well as others will never be known. The sand ridge and netted gourd are significant when referring to the primeval mound of the Egyptian Temple (mound of the First Time) and the net when referring back to the Edfu net. Transcribing this ceremony in the end notes in no way reveals its inner secrets. One can see something hidden in plain sight yet not know its significance. Anthropological methods follow a rigorous path in recording every detail yet unless you are born in that society and initiated, the anthropologist will always be missing the "ignition key")

12 Armin W. Geertz, "Hopi Indian Altar Iconography", Iconography of Religions, Institute of Religious Iconography State University Groningen, Section X: North America, Fascicle Five, 1987, page 14.
13 Ibid, page 14.
14 Ibid, page 27.
15 Ibid, page 14.
16 H.R. Voth, :Notes on Modern Burial Customs", Field Museum of natural History, Publication 157, Anthropological series Vol. XI, No. 2, Chicago, February 1912, pages 102-103.
17 Ibid, page 103.
18 E.A. Wallis Budge, "The Gods of the Egyptians", Vol. 1, pages 333-334.

19 H.P. Mera, "Pueblo Designs", page 6.

20 Ibid, page 7.

21 E.A.E. Reymond, "The Mythical Origin of the Egyptian Temple", page 14.

22 Ibid, page 7.

23 Ibid, page 15.

24 Ibid, page 17.

25 Ibid, pages 198, 138.

26 Ibid, page 28.

27 Ibid, page 13.

28 Ibid, page 13.

29 Ibid, page 122.

30 Ibid, pages 123-124.

31 Frank Waters, "Book of the Hopi", pages 18-19.

32 Dennis Slifer and James Duffield, Kokopelli, page 4.

33 E.A.E. Reymond, "The Mythical Origin of the Egyptian Temple", page 213.

34 Ibid, pages 30-31.

35 Ibid, page 262.

36 R.O. Falkner, "The Ancient Egyptian Pyramid Texts", Utterances 723, 738, 442.

37 James Reston JT, "Orion: Where Stars are Born" National Geographic, December 1995, page 95.

38 E.A.E. Reymond, "The Mythical Origin of the Egyptian Temple", page 278.

39 Ibid, page 236.

40 Ibid, pages 314-315.

41 Ibid, page 294.

42 A.M. Blackman and H.W. Fairman, "The Consecration of an Egyptian Temble According to the use of Edfu, JEA, XXXII (1946).

43 Robert Bauval and Adrian Gilbert, "The Orion Mystery", page 206.

44 Ibid, page 206.

45 Ibid, page 209.

46 Ibid, page 208.

47 Ronald Goodman, "Lakota Star Knowledge" Appendix F, page 57.

48 Wallace H. Clack Elk and William S. Lyon, "Black Elk", page 51.

Chapter Three

1   Murry Hope, "The Sirius Connection", Fig. 11.1, page 182.
2   Frank Waters, "Book of the Hopi", page 223.
3   Ibid, page 223.
4   Helga Teiwes, "Hopi Basket Weaving", page 146.
5   Ibid, page 158.
6   Frank Waters, "Book of the Hopi", page 23.
7   Helga Teiwes, "Hopi Basket Weaving", page 156.
8   Frank Waters, "Book of the Hopi", pages 128-129.
9   Ibid, page 129.
10 Ruth F. Kirk, "Zuni Fetishism", pages 3-4: "Cushing speculates on a possible evolution from the round to the square, concluding it was effected by the semi-settled western starin that intermingled with the cliff dwelling people." Possibly, but the explanation does not address to why.
11 Fred Alan Wolf, "The Eagle's Quest", page 203.
12 Ibid, Chapter 9.
13 Ibid, page 207.
14 Ibid, page 105.
15 Graham Hancock, "The Sign and the Seal", Chapter 13, Treasures of Darkness, page 348. Though Graham does not specifically mention radioactive material specifically "a potent and durable source of energy" which fits nicely with nuclear substances which are potent (radioactive) and durable (having a very long half life). As well, the Guardian was mentioned as having cataracts-a known symptom of being exposed to radiation. Huge amounts of frankincense is burned in the church; frankincense puts out a huge amount of smoke (carbon) which could be acting as a moderator, shielding the Ark's power.
16 Col. Phillip J. Corso (Ret.), "The Day after Roswell", page 188.

Chapter Four

1   Graham Hancock and Santha Faiia, "Heaven's Mirror", page 316.
2   Ibid, page 316.
3   Michael Harner, "The Way of the Shaman", page 4.

4   H.R. Voth, "The Oraibi Summer Snake Ceremony", Field Columbian Museum, Publication No. 83, Anthropological Series, Vol. III, No. 4, Chicago, U.S.A., November, 1903, page 342.

5   Ibid, pages 341-342.

6   Murry Hope, "The Sirius Connection", Fig. 11.1, page 182.

Chapter Five

1   Center of Documentation and Studies on Ancient Egypt, Center of Documentation Press, pages 8-9.

2   Fred Alan Wolf, "Parallel Universes, The Search for Other Worlds", page 167.

3   Ibid, pages 166-168.

4   Stephen Hawkins, "The Large Scale Structure of Space-Time".

5   Fred Alan Wolf, Parallel Universes, "The Search for other Worlds", page 143.

6   Aryeh Kaplan, "Sefer Yetzirah, the Book of Creation", page 31.

7   Dr. Paul Brunton, "A Search in Secret Egypt", page 180.

8   Ibid, page 180.

9   Murry Hope, "The Sirius Connection", page 171.

10   E.A. Wallis Budge, "the Gods of the Egyptians", Volume 1, page 407.

11   Ibid, page 406.

12   Armin W. Geertz, "Hopi Indian Altar", Iconography, page 19.

13   Ibid, page 19.

14   E.A. Wallis Budge, "The Gods of the Egyptians", Vol. 1, page 406.

15   Aryeh Kaplan, "Sefer Yetzirah, The Book of Creation", pages 79-80.

16   Ibid, page 78.

17   Ibid, page 78.

18   Isha Schwaller De Lubicz, "Her-Bak, Egyptian Initiate, page 357.

Chapter Six

1   E.A. Wallis Budge, "Egyptian Ideas of the Afterlife" quoting Receuil de Travaux, Tom. Iv. P. 71 (1.582)., page 167.

2   E.A. Wallis Budge, "Egyptian Magic", page 182.

3   E.A. Wallis Budge, "The Gods of the Egyptians", Volume 2, page 128.

4   Ibid.

5   E.A. Wallis Budge, "The Gods of the Egyptians, Volume 1, page 505.

6   E.A. Wallis Budge, "The Gods of the Egyptians", Volume 2, page 130.

7   R.A. Schwaller De Lubicz, "Sacred Science", page 216.

8   R.O. Falkner, "The Ancient Egyptian Pyramid Texts", Utterance 356,text 578-579, page 114.

9   R.A. Schwaller De Lubicz, "Sacred Science", page 217.

10 Isha Schwaller De Lubicz, "Her-Bak Egyptian Initiate", page 190.

11 Ibid, page 192.

12 R.A. Schwaller De Lubicz, "sacred Science", page 218.

13 Isha Schwaller De Lubicz, "Her-Bak Egyptian Initiate", pages 361-362.

14 Ibid, page 350.

15 Ibid, page 283.

16 Jacqueline I. Kroschwitz, Melvin Winokur, "Chemistry, General Organic, Biological", page 569.

17 Ibid.

18 M.-W. Ho and F.-A. Popp, "Biological Organization, Coherence, & Light Emission" from "Thinking about Biology", edited by Wilfred Stein & Francisco J. Varela, page 207.

19 Ibid.

20 Ibid.

21 Ibid, pages 207-208.

22 Ibid, page 209.

23 Bob Brier, "Egyptian Mummies", page 191.

24 Ibid, page 190.

25 Isha Schwaller De Lubicz, "Her-Bak Egyptian Initiate", page 361.

Chapter Seven

1   Alice Bryant and Phylis Galde, "The message of the Crystal Skull From Atlantis to the New Age, Page 142.

2   Chris Morton and Ceri Louise Thomas, "The Mystery of the Crystal Skull" page 274.

3   Barbara Watterson, "The House of Horus at Edfu, Ritual in an Ancient Egyptian Temple, page 36.

4   Alice Bryant and Phylis Galde, "The Message of the Crystal Skull From Atlantis to the New Age", page 142.

5   R.O. Falkner, "The Ancient Egyptian Pyramid Texts", Utterance 519, page 192.

6   Ibid, Utterance 473, page 161.

7   Barbara Watterson, "The House of Horus at Edfu, Ritual in an Ancient Egyptian Temple, Chapter 12.

8   Graham Hancock, "Fingerprints of the Gods", Pages 377-378.

9   Graham Hancock and Robert Bauval, "The Message of the Sphinx, a Quest for the Hidden Legacy of Mankind", page 108.

10 Aiden Dodson, "The Canopic Equipment of the Kings of Egypt", page 5.

11 Ibid, page 5.

12 Ibid, page 10.

13 Ibid, page 10.